Self-Discovery and Authority
in Afro-American Narrative

Self-Discovery and Authority in Afro-American Narrative

VALERIE SMITH

HARVARD UNIVERSITY PRESS
CAMBRIDGE, MASSACHUSETTS
AND LONDON, ENGLAND

Copyright © 1987 by the President and Fellows of Harvard College
All rights reserved
Printed in the United States of America
10 9 8 7 6 5 4 3 2

First Harvard University Press paperback edition, 1991

Library of Congress Cataloging-in-Publication Data

Smith, Valerie, 1956–
    Self-discovery and authority in Afro-American
narrative.

    Bibliography: p.
    Includes index.
    1. American fiction—Afro-American authors—History
and criticism.   2. American fiction—20th century—
History and criticism.   3. Afro-Americans in literature.
4. Self in literature.   5. Authority in literature.
6. American prose literature—Afro-American authors—
History and criticism.   7. Afro-Americans—Biography—
History and criticism.   8. Slaves—United States—
Biography—History and criticism.   9. Literacy—
United States.   10. Slavery and slaves in literature.
11. Narration (Rhetoric)   12. Autobiography.   I. Title.
PS153.N5S63   1987   813'.009'896073   87-11950
ISBN 0-674-80087-7 (alk. paper) (cloth)
ISBN 0-674-80088-5 (paper)

For W. Reeves and Josephine Irving Smith

Acknowledgments

This book would never have been completed without the financial support of several institutions and the advice and encouragement of advisers, colleagues, friends, and relatives during the stages of its development. As a dissertation, the project was funded generously by the National Fellowships Fund of the Ford Foundation and the W. E. B. Du Bois Institute for Afro-American Studies Research at Harvard University. Princeton University, the Surdna Foundation, and the Mary Ingraham Bunting Institute of Radcliffe College financed my time away from teaching so that I could complete revisions of the manuscript. I am particularly grateful to Margaret McKenna, Ann Bookman, and the staff of the Bunting Institute for allowing me the opportunity to spend my year's leave in a scholarly, feminist, supportive community.

Raymond J. Nelson and Alan B. Howard of the English department at the University of Virginia directed this project when it was a dissertation, and offered wise counsel and guidance. At Princeton Emory Elliott, William Howarth, James H. Kavanagh, A. Walton Litz, Elaine Showalter, Sally Shuttleworth, and David Van Leer read sections or drafts of the work and made valuable, timely suggestions. I am indebted to friends and colleagues at the Bunting Institute—

Marianne Hirsch, Gail T. Reimer, Susan Strasser, and Iréne Sosa Vásquez—who inspired me to refine the focus of the book. And I wish to thank my editor at Harvard University Press, Margaretta Fulton, for her patience and vision.

I would like to acknowledge a number of scholars of Afro-American literature who read versions of the work during the past several years, challenged its assumptions, and offered encouragement when most I needed it: Arlene Clift-Pellow, Henry Louis Gates, Jr., Barbara Johnson, Nellie Y. McKay, Robert J. O'Meally, Werner Sollors, Mary Helen Washington, and Richard Yarborough.

Finally, I thank my brother, Daryl, my sister, Vera, and most especially my parents, W. Reeves and Josephine Irving Smith, for their confidence in this book and their unwavering love for me. Because they have repeatedly given me the courage to face whatever overwhelms, to them should go the credit for this project, and to them this book is dedicated.

ૐ

An early version of chapter 5 appeared in *The Southern Review* as "The Quest for and Discovery of Identity in Toni Morrison's *Song of Solomon,*" 21 (Summer 1985), 721–732.

I wish to thank Alfred A. Knopf, Inc., for permission to quote from *The Autobiography of an Ex-Colored Man,* copyright © 1927, 1951, 1955 by James Weldon Johnson, *Song of Solomon,* copyright © 1977 by Toni Morrison, and *Sula,* copyright © 1973 by Toni Morrison; Random House, Inc., for permission to quote from *Invisible Man,* copyright © 1947, 1948, 1952 by Ralph Ellison; and Henry Holt and Company, Inc., for permission to quote from *The Bluest Eye,* copyright © 1970 by Toni Morrison. I also wish to thank Harper and Row, Jonathan Cape, Ltd., and Mrs. Ellen Wright for permission to quote from *Native Son,* copyright © 1940 by Richard Wright.

Contents

Introduction   I

1. Form and Ideology in Three Slave Narratives   9

2. Privilege and Evasion in *The Autobiography*
   of an Ex-Colored Man   44

3. Alienation and Creativity in the Fiction
   of Richard Wright   65

4. Ralph Ellison's Invisible Autobiographer   88

5. Toni Morrison's Narratives of Community   122

Notes   155

Index   165

*Self-Discovery and Authority
in Afro-American Narrative*

Introduction

Frederick Douglass's 1845 autobiography, *The Narrative of the Life of Frederick Douglass, An American Slave, Written by Himself,* has been the point of departure for numerous critical studies of Afro-American literature. It owes its importance in part to the subtlety of the narrative voice: Douglass's ability to counterpoise his perceptions as a young slave with his analyses as a seasoned writer prefigures the cultural doubleness that W. E. B. Du Bois and other black American writers have described. And in part, the text enjoys particular prominence because it is the most carefully crafted example of the slave narrative, the earliest genre in which large numbers of Afro-Americans wrote and the common point of origin of much black fictional and nonfictional prose.

If Douglass's *Narrative* is the referent to which dozens of later black narratives look back, then the cluster of scenes in which his autobiographical persona learns to read is the one which is most frequently echoed. By representing the tension between his desire to read and his master's objection to his education, Douglass captures the distance between the interests of black subordinate and white superordinate. Moreover, when he links the acquisition of literacy to the process of liberation, he forges a connection that resonates for subsequent generations of writers.

As early as 1829, in his *Appeal in Four Articles,* David Walker spoke of the transforming power of education: "For colored people to acquire learning in this country, makes tyrants quake and tremble on their sandy foundation."[1] As if to elaborate on this notion, Douglass remarks that learning to read and write provides "the pathway from slavery to freedom."[2] Almost a century later, Richard Wright attributes his resistance to authority to the fact that reading introduced him to alternate ways of living. Maya Angelou suggests that the discovery of literature freed her from the traumatic aftereffects of an episode of sexual molestation. And Malcolm X links his mental acuity to his rediscovery of reading during his jail term.

This book has grown out of my efforts to understand both the influence of the slave narratives on later black writing and the variety of ways in which the idea of literacy is used within the tradition of Afro-American letters. I argue here that slave narrators and the protagonist-narrators of certain twentieth-century novels by Afro-American writers affirm and legitimize their psychological autonomy by telling the stories of their own lives. My work centers on the paradox that by fictionalizing one's life, one bestows a quality of authenticity on it. My analyses show that the processes of plot construction, characterization, and designation of beginnings and endings—in short the process of authorship—provide the narrators with a measure of authority unknown to them in either real or fictional life. The narrators not only grant themselves significance and figurative power over their superordinates, but in their manipulation of received literary conventions they also engage with and challenge the dominant ideology.

It should not surprise us that Afro-American writers traditionally have attached great significance to the acts of reading and writing. Since an unlettered slave was assumed to be ignorant and easy to dominate, antebellum laws privileged the acquisition of letters by explicitly prohibiting slaves from being taught to read and write. This prohibition implied, for example, that slaves who could not write would not be able to write their own passes, and that slaves who could not read would be unable to challenge their masters' scriptural sanctions of slavery. Similarly equating literacy with freedom, writers such as the ones cited previously have identified their spiritual and intellectual rebirth with the moment when they learned to read.

In a self-pitying, condescending passage Frederick Douglass longs to return to his earlier unlettered state, when he was content to be a slave: "[Learning to read] opened my eyes to the horrible pit, but to no ladder upon which to get out. In moments of agony, I envied my fellow slaves for their stupidity. I have often wished myself a beast. I preferred the condition of the meanest reptile to my own. Any thing, no matter what, to get rid of thinking!" (p. 67). Douglass's juxtapositions—his yearning to be, in rapid succession, an ignorant slave, a beast, a reptile—reveal his acceptance of the Western assumption that the use of language distinguishes human from animal life. Without letters, Douglass suggests, the slave is "rid of thinking," is hardly higher than a beast. Moreover, he assumes that he yearns to be free only because he has read of freedom and abolition in such texts as "The Columbian Orator" and Sheridan's speeches on Catholic emancipation. He, like the slave owner, suggests that without letters, slaves fail to understand the full meaning of their domination.

There must be some truth to the formulations of Douglass, Angelou, Wright, and the rest, for in our literate culture success is in large measure linked to one's ability to read and write the official language. But since the time of the Roman state, literacy has been a tool of social organization and control, inspiring in the learner a respect for authority. The ability to read and write thus does not in and of itself guarantee freedom and sophistication of expression; the very structures of discourse themselves embody values and assumptions that may elude one's control. Letters, in other words, do not the intellect make. Douglass, Wright, Angelou, Malcolm X, and others might have found that literacy, narrowly defined, developed and organized their thoughts, but as Robert Pattison has written, "Literacy did not—does not ever by itself—awaken the passion of the mind."[3]

I have found Pattison's radical critique of Western notions of literacy useful. He demonstrates that to link reading and writing inextricably with social development is to display an inherent bias toward Anglo-American uses of language; to his mind literacy might be defined more broadly as the consciousness of the uses and problems of language, whether spoken or written. From his perspective it is thus only "secondarily a skill in the technologies, such as rhetoric and writing, by which this consciousness is expressed."[4] In this view the unlettered person who can manipulate the meanings and nuances of the spoken word might also be considered literate.

As many slave narrators and historians such as John Blassingame and Vincent Harding have shown, scores of unlettered blacks stole away from their enslavement without benefit of books that explained the meaning of freedom.[5] I would suggest that they as much as, if not more than, blacks who wrote accounts of their bondage and escape demonstrate the link between language and power. If we are to believe the historians and the narrators, the slaves' survival depended in large measure on their behaving in accordance with their masters' expectations. The figure of the docile, singing, pious, cheerful slave led slavery's apologists, and some twentieth-century historians, to assume that blacks enjoyed their captivity. But innumerable recorded and unrecorded cases indicate that slaves about to become fugitives often affected obedience in order to win their masters' trust and take advantage of their leniency. Their superficial docility masked independence of mind and resourcefulness; like anyone oppressed because of race, class, or gender, they learned to read their superordinates' expectations while themselves remaining inscrutable. Whether possessed of book learning or not, the dissembling slave was a confidence figure who displayed a profound consciousness of language, created a space for the expression of his or her will or identity, and seized the opportunity to escape.

By examining autobiography as process rather than genre, I seek to question the significance of book learning in the black text. I argue that the narrators master their subject by imposing narrative order upon it; this privilege results from the ability to manipulate language whether orally or in writing. In this light the oral accounts of Wright's Bigger Thomas (discussed in chapter 3) and Morrison's Milkman Dead (discussed in chapter 5) are seen to be gestures of liberation equivalent to the written narratives of the former slaves, Johnson's ex-colored man, or Ellison's unnamed protagonist.

&

This book is as much about its method as it is about its explicit subject. It grows out of my efforts to find a mode of critical inquiry that might allow me to analyze the figurative dimension of a text within the context of the conditions of its production. The techniques of close reading in which I was trained do much to illuminate the construction of a piece of writing. Yet they foster a kind of textual elitism that devalues considerations of historical or biographical context. They suggest that our understanding of a work of literature might be enhanced by reference to other imaginative works from the same genre, period, or great tradition, but they minimize its relation to contemporaneous economic and political theory and to historical developments. As Terry Eagleton, Frank Lentricchia, and other ideological critics have argued, such ostensible efforts to rarefy or purify the literary and critical enterprises carry their own political agenda.[6] The renunciation of the privilege to challenge or engage with the dominant ideology may seem to be apolitical, but the mere refusal to engage actually strengthens the dominant ideology.

That conservatism so easily masquerades as neutrality should at least give us pause before we undertake any formalist or purely textual analysis. But ahistorical readings pose special problems for the critic of Afro-American writing. All literature bears the imprint of the writer's experience of society; black American writing, arising as it does from an experience alien to mainstream American culture, has tended by and large to articulate the writer's experience of de jure or de facto subordination. The political and economic context in which the texts have been produced has undeniably inscribed itself in their rhetorical structures. Thus to analyze the texts without reference to the broad context in which they were written invites misreading and denies their relation to the conditions and the sense of urgency that contributed to their very existence. Furthermore, to emphasize the textual dimension is to misrepresent the complex origins and affinities of the black work of literature. Afro-American writers draw on both an oral and a literate tradition; their debts to the one influence shape them and distance them from the other. To focus on the texts' literariness, then, is to oversimplify their lineage, and to pay homage to the structures of discourse that so often contributed to the writers' oppression.

As Henry Louis Gates, Jr., reminds us, however, a work

of literature is not transparent.[7] A figurative construction, it does not exist as a one-way mirror on history or biography. What it means (or what it intends to mean) is linked inextricably to the way it embodies meaning; we can discern its politics and its relation to ideology only through close analysis of its language. Thus, to restate its self-consciously polemical statements, to rely on sweeping thematic generalizations alone, or to read plot and character oversimply in terms of biographical and historical parallels does a disservice to both its figurative and political dimensions. If, however, we take as our point of departure the textual status of a work and examine the way it engages with, challenges, and transforms narrative conventions and the politics they enshrine, we can arrive at a fuller understanding of its rhetorical achievement and the complexity of its ideology. In other words, the critical work, no less than the artistic, bears the imprint of the conditions under which it was produced and articulates the writer's relation to culture. To assume the inseparability of political and figurative discourse enables the critic both to engage in elaborate analytic operations on a text, and to link that analysis to the writer's experience of society.

This study lacks the analysis of broad historical and political forces that I advocate in these prefatory remarks. The selection of texts from disparate historical periods has rendered such thorough contextualization unfeasible. To guard against the kind of textual elitism of which I speak, however, I have employed an eclectic method in order to provide some sense of the literary-historical conditions that gave rise to the works in question. I therefore place my readings of Equiano's, Douglass's, and Jacobs's accounts in the context of a discussion of the complex generic situation in which they were produced. I explore ways in which the fictional autobiographies of Johnson and Ellison invoke and subvert the form of this most American of genres. And I show that the oral accounts of Wright's Bigger and Morrison's Milkman can be comprehended fully only when considered in relation to the meaning of voice and narration established in the authors' earlier works.

ONE

Form and Ideology in Three Slave Narratives

The way in which the narratives of freed and fugitive slaves were produced has been largely responsible for their uncertain status as subjects of critical inquiry. In form they most closely resemble autobiographies. But if we expect autobiographies to present us with rhetorical figures and thematic explorations that reveal the author's sense of what his or her life means, then these stories disappoint. In each stage of their history, the presence of an intermediary renders the majority of the narratives not artistic constructions of personal experience but illustrations of someone else's view of slavery.

In the earliest examples of the genre, as William L. Andrews has shown, the relationship between narrator and text was triangulated through the ordering intelligence of a white amanuensis or editor. Relying on a model of slavery as a fundamentally benevolent institution, the early narratives portray the slave as either an outlaw or a wayfarer in need of the protection that only white paternal authority could provide.[1] Most of the middle-period accounts, published from the 1830s through the 1860s, claim to be written by the narrators themselves, yet these cases too serve an outside interest: the stories are shaped according to the requirements of the abolitionists who published them and provided them with readers. And as Marion Wilson Starling and Dorothy Sterling have acknowledged, even the narratives transcribed in the twentieth century by the Federal Writers' Project of the Works Progress Administration (WPA) bear more than their share of the interviewers' influence.[2] As Sterling remarks:

> Few of the interviewers were linguists. They transcribed the ex-slaves' speech as they heard it, as they thought they heard it, or as they thought it should have been said—and sometimes, the whiter the interviewer's skin, the heavier the dialect and the more erratic the spelling. A number of the interviews also went through an editorial process in which dialect was cleaned up or exaggerated, depending on the editors' judgment. To attempt to make the language of the interviews consistent or to "translate" them into standard English would add still another change.[3]

It is not surprising that a scholarly tradition that values the achievements of the classically educated, middle-class white male has dismissed the transcriptions of former slaves' oral accounts. Nor is it surprising that even those narratives that purport to be written by slaves themselves have come into disrepute: when three popular narratives were exposed as inauthentic between 1836 and 1838, serious doubts arose about authorship in the genre as a whole.[4] But the intrusive abolitionist influence has interfered with the critical reception of even those narratives that are demonstrably genuine. The former slaves may have seized upon the writing of their life stories as an opportunity to celebrate their escape and to reveal the coherence and meaning of their lives. These personal motives notwithstanding, the narratives were also (if not primarily) literary productions that documented the antislavery crusade. Their status as both popular art and propaganda imposed upon them a repetitiveness of structure, tone, and content that obscured individual achievements and artistic merit.[5]

As Henry Louis Gates, Jr., has shown, apologists and detractors alike have failed to attend to the formal dimensions of black texts:

> For all sorts of complex historical reasons, the very act of writing has been a "political" act for the black author. Even our most solipsistic texts, at least since the Enlightenment in Europe, have been treated as political evidence of one sort or another both implicitly and explicitly. And because our life in the West has been one struggle after another, our literature has been defined from without, and rather often from within, as primarily just one more polemic in those struggles.[6]

The formulaic and hybrid quality of the narratives has rendered their status as critical subjects even more elusive than that of other examples of Afro-American literary expression. Combining elements of history, autobiography, and fiction, they raise unique questions of interpretation. To study them as, for example, sustained images of an author's experience ignores the fact that they conform rather programmatically to a conventional pattern. Or to talk about the unity of an individual narrative is to ignore the fact that the texts as we read them contain numerous authenticating documents that create a panoply of other voices. Only by beginning from a clear sense of the narratives' generic properties does one capture the subtlety and achievement of the most compelling accounts.[7]

The narratives discussed here elude the domination of received generic structures and conventions. Douglass's *Narrative of the Life of Frederick Douglass, An American Slave, Written by Himself* (1845) certainly achieves this kind of autonomy; I also include in this category Equiano's account, *The Interesting Narrative of the Life of Olaudah Equiano, or Gustavus Vassa, the African, Written by Himself* (1789), and Harriet Jacobs's *Incidents in the Life of a Slave Girl* (1861). As my formulation implies, my interest is both aesthetic and political. The narratives that test the limits of the formula tell us most about what those conventions signify. Furthermore, the narrators who transform the conventions into an image of what they believe their lives mean most closely resemble autobiographers; they leave the impress of their personal experience on the structure in which they tell their story. Perhaps most important, these narratives are of interest because in their variations on the formula they provide a figure for the author's liberation from slavery, the central act of the accounts themselves. In these places of difference, the narrators of these stories of freedom reveal their resistance even to the domination of their white allies.

સ⬩

Equiano's *Life* shares with other early narratives a relatively mild vision of slavery. As several critics have noted, the earliest accounts are essentially records of the authors' lives and experiences as slaves that include descriptions of the structure and practices of slavery.[8] Only with the rise of the antislavery influence and the passage of increasingly stringent legislation that rendered the institution even more inhumane did the narratives begin to stress its brutality and demand its abolition.

As Andrews has shown, the early narrators tended to choose one of two ways to represent the meaning of slavery in their lives.[9] Some, like Joseph Mountain, Arthur, Edmund Fortis, and Stephen Smith, followed the model of the popular criminal-confession narratives; others, like James Gronniosaw, George White, and Equiano, imitated the structure of the conversion narrative. The black criminal confessions identify the slaves' misfortune with their yearning for autonomy and feature slavery as a set of benevolent controls: "The average black criminal narrative is the story of a young man whose break with the authority figures in his life is presented as a symbol of his willful contempt for all systems of ordering and restraining the self."[10] The black conversion narratives likewise appropriated a rhetoric that denies the value of independence of mind and will. Moreover, their view of human existence as a drama of suffering that earns one a heavenly reward forestalled any questioning of slavery's injustices. The two forms thus either extol or deemphasize the impact of slavery in the life of the individual and minimize the writer-protagonist's significance and power.

In part because of his allegiance to both the Africa of his birth and the Europe and North America of his enslavement and choice, Equiano resists the ideological implications of the form of the conversion narrative in which he writes. Inscribed throughout his narrative, in his juxtapositions and in the modulations of his voice, is a simultaneous adoption of and withdrawal from the assumptions that inform the conventions of his genre. Equiano's narrative retains a quality of doubleness that correlates with the complex interrelation between his origins and socialization. That duplicity makes possible his authority over his form and its implicit ideology.

In his "Dedication," Equiano prepares his reader for the story of a life indebted to God's grace, an account that owes much to the structure and rhetoric of the conversion narrative. He writes: "By the horrors of [the slave trade] was I first torn away from all the tender connections that were naturally dear to my heart; but these, through the mysterious ways of Providence, I ought to regard as infinitely more than compensated by the introduction I have thence obtained to the knowledge of the Christian religion, and of a nation which . . . has exalted the dignity of human nature."[11] The passage features Providence as both the source of meaning and the central figure in the narrator's life, for it juxtaposes his naive misperceptions with the insights he attributes to God's grace. What he once saw as "horrors" and sufferings have been revealed as blessings in the course of time.

The ensuing narrative elaborates on this early allusion to the providential influence. Repeatedly Equiano invokes the presence of God's controlling hand in even the most insignificant circumstances. When, for example, his captain forbids him to bring aboard ship a set of bullocks he hopes to sell in foreign markets, Equiano is disappointed that he will have to settle for turkeys, less valuable livestock. On this voyage, however, all the bullocks and the captain himself die, while Equiano's turkeys survive and bring him a considerable price. What might appear coincidental to another imagination provides Equiano with evidence of God's benevolence. Of the captain's death he remarks, "Had it pleased Providence that [the captain] had died but five months before, I verily believed I should not have obtained my freedom when I did, and . . . I might not have been able to get it . . . afterwards" (p. 135). Of the episode generally he writes, "I could not help looking upon this . . . circumstance, as a particular providence of God; and was accordingly thankful" (p. 135).

Equiano shares with other spiritual autobiographers this tendency to view the quotidian symbolically. More important, his treatment of his own conversion resembles the way this event is presented elsewhere in the genre. The process of his conversion follows the stages other narrators describe; it occupies as theirs do the thematic center of his account. He describes first an early transformation that initiates him into "easy self-righteousness" but not "the new birth of saving grace."[12] His authentic conversion, however, possesses like theirs a transcendent quality: the Lord appears to him in visions and voices and answers his supplications with specific instructions. Immediately after this transformation occurs, he endures a period of discouragement, a sense of his own inadequacy, from which he learns that grace, not works, is responsible for his salvation. This realization brings him profound joy and peace such as had been unknown to him previously. It provides the lens through which he reassesses past experiences and appreciates those to come, and it is the source of the tone, rhetoric, and imagery of his narration.[13]

But if Equiano's debt to the plot of the conversion narrative is clear, that is not his only story; his second story is the one told by the other voice in the text, the voice that jars during even a superficial reading of the account and that has been the focus of critical commentary.[14] Most of the narrative is told from Equiano's reasoned, equable, and worldly wise adult point of view. This tone, however, is interrupted on several occasions in the first third of the book by his uninitiated, naive point of view as a young African boy, as in the following excerpt:

> The first object that saluted my eyes when I arrived on the coast was the sea, and a slave ship . . . These filled me with astonishment, that was soon converted into terror, which I am yet at a loss to describe . . . I was immediately handled and tossed up to see if I was sound, by some of the crew; and I was now persuaded that I had got into a world of bad spirits, and that they were going to kill me. Their complexions too, differing so much from ours, their long hair, and the language they spoke, which was very different from any I had ever heard, united to confirm me in this belief. (p. 31)

In the first sentence he speaks from an adult perspective, the point of view of a man with sufficient experience to call a slave ship by name. But immediately thereafter he envelops his readers in his innocent perspective so that we witness his terror at seeing for the first time the sea, a ship, a race of men who look and sound nothing like him. His use of this technique operates at several levels and allows him to manipulate his relationship to his reader and to the form in which he writes.

At the most superficial level Equiano seems in this passage to ridicule his own ignorance and ally himself with his more sophisticated reader. But this interpretation assumes a capacity for self-loathing, a sense of distance from his African past, that belies the immediacy of his opening description of his beloved homeland. Not only does he describe the Africa of his childhood in utopian terms, as the following passage suggests, but he also clearly considers himself still an African: "We are almost a nation of dancers, musicians, and poets. Every great event, such as a triumphant return from battle . . . is celebrated in public dances" (p. 5). Rather than ridiculing his own naiveté, then, Equiano might be said to be introducing his youthful voice at least in part to underscore the process of his remarkable development. By showing his progress from childhood timidity to adult wisdom and courage, he dramatizes his exceptional nature and, alternatively, the miraculous workings of Providence.

At yet another level Equiano uses this technique as a means of commenting ironically on the ostensibly civilized nature of his European captors (and, by extension, readers). On the one hand he encourages us to consider his unjustified terror at the sight of the ship and of white men. But on the other hand, after he describes the conditions on the slave ship, he reminds us that in fact the vessel and those who operate it are the repository and the perpetrators, respectively, of inexpressible savageries: "When I looked round the ship too, and saw a large furnace or copper boiling, and a multitude of black people, of every description, chained together, every one of their countenances expressing dejection and sorrow, I no longer doubted of my fate" (p. 32). This juxtaposition suggests that Equiano manipulates the mask of naiveté to cover a scathing denunciation of European inhumanity. Precisely at the moment when he appears to embrace the reader, he issues a subtle indictment.

Most important, however, by introducing the voice of his youth and naiveté, Equiano gives credibility to his African origins, his pre-European consciousness. His commentary—reminding the reader of the influence of Providence—suggests that his conversion bestows upon his life its true meaning. But finally that voice does not fully usurp the emphasis from his prior perceptions. Rather, by showing that his imagination and perspective bear the indelible impress of his African origins, he demonstrates as well that only as an African does he understand and value Christianity, seizing upon it as the single feature of European society that restores the metaphysical certainty he lost when he was enslaved.[15]

To Equiano, Benin, the province in which he was born, represents an Edenic civilization, a world rich in natural resources and inhabited by industrious, reverent, contented people. He attributes the quality of life there to its orderliness: age-old, straightforward, consistent, and reasonable economic, legal, and religious customs prevail; unencumbered by superfluity of any kind, they guarantee a continued correspondence between part and whole, past and present, cause and effect. Throughout his description he emphasizes the efficiency of cultural practice in his homeland, remarking, for example, that "the history of what passes in one family or village, may serve as a specimen of the whole nation" (p. 3). Perhaps the most striking correspondence exists between word and deed. A person's name commemorates an event that marks his or her birth in some way; and people dare not blaspheme for fear of invoking their God's presence and wrath. In such a stable community an individual's status is determined by his or her place in the family and the family's social position; Equiano therefore knew even as a child that he, like his father and brother, was destined to wear the "Embrenche," or mark of distinction.

Given his idyllic representation of Benin, his abduction into slavery seems to be his introduction into temporality and human fallibility. Indeed, his points of emphasis throughout the narrative suggest that he considers slavery's greatest injustice to be the fact that it renders the slave's fate capricious, a matter entirely of his or her master's whim. Not only does he associate his first experience of suffering with his captivity, but it also precipitates his initial awareness that neither word and deed nor cause and effect need correspond according to his expectations. The Europeans' casual use of language thus disturbs him: he resists his masters' cavalier efforts to change his name, and is distressed by the freedom with which people blaspheme. He repeatedly remarks upon the discrepancy between his expectations of a situation and its actual outcome. Even when he describes specific sorrows, he emphasizes not the intensity of his sufferings but rather the fact that they are unexpected.

Just before he embarks on the dread Middle Passage, for example, he spends two months in the service of a wealthy widow and her son. He is only nominally enslaved by this family, who treat him as an equal, providing him with his own slaves. Just as Equiano has settled into his comfortable life, however, he is sold to slave traders. It is clear that his experience on the ship is devastating, but he is disturbed as much by its unexpectedness as by the experience itself: "Without the least previous knowledge, one morning early

. . . I was awakened out of my reverie to fresh sorrow, and was hurried away even among the uncircumcised. *Thus, at the very moment I dreamed of the greatest happiness, I found myself most miserable;* and it seemed as if fortune wished to give me this taste of joy only to render the reverse more poignant" (pp. 28–29; emphasis mine).

Equiano appears to value the certainty of order in his life and laments its disruption. It is thus little wonder that he celebrates the ability of Christianity to offer him a context that attributes each event in his life to a First Cause. As he remarks during the account of his conversion: "Now every leading providential circumstance that happened to me, from the day that I was taken from my parents to that hour, was then in my view, as if it had just then occurred. I was sensible of the invisible hand of God, which guided and protected me, when in truth I knew it not" (p. 189). Events that seemed most inexplicable, such as his initial abduction, he can now interpret as a step in a divine plan whose meaningfulness he can trust even when it appears inscrutable.

What is remarkable about this formulation is that it constitutes a subtle revision of the conversion plot. Like other spiritual autobiographers, Equiano is quite willing to count as nothing his early life of self-righteousness. But the fact that he preserves the voice of his personal innocence and insightfulness and the image of an African paradise suggests his unwillingness to yield himself entirely to the religion and practices of his adopted country. No doubt he reveres the European's Christianity, but he presents it as his way of recovering a lost ideal and shows how it suits a system of values and priorities conditioned by African cultural practice.

His use of the double narrative voice, then, both unites him with and differentiates him from his reader. The prevailing mature voice articulates his acceptance of the values of his adoptive nation. The voice of his African boyhood remains, however, reminding his reader always that he filters, understands, and appropriates his new religion and culture from the point of view of an outsider.

ૐ

If the double voice of Equiano's narrative symbolizes his allegiance to both his African heritage and his European acculturation, it allows him as well to adopt a critical stance toward the capacity for savagery of a society he otherwise admires. In other words, his ability to celebrate Western scientific advances does not prevent him from denouncing the brutality of the slave trade and its casual treatment of human life. Likewise, his love of Christianity does not blind him to the fact that self-professed Christians are capable of greater abuses than anyone he knew in his putatively heathen homeland. This indictment prefigures the distinction between the slaveholders' religion and the true religion drawn by countless later slave narrators.

Frederick Douglass's *Narrative* shares with Equiano's this quality of doubleness. Both writers are simultaneously complicit with and critical of the ideology of those who dominate them. Equiano's account proclaims his debt to Western civilization while suggesting his distance from it. But partly because of changes in the nature of slavery, Douglass and his contemporaries (such as Henry Bibb, Henry Box Brown, William Wells Brown, Moses Grandy, Solomon Northup, J. W. C. Pennington, and Moses Roper) were able to express their contempt for the institution. If Douglass's narrative articulates an antislavery position in terms that are sufficiently recognizable to seem formulaic, he recounts as well, and perhaps with greater resonance than any of his counterparts, his personal story of an individual who remains unbroken by his experience as a slave. The very terms in which he casts his self-presentation, however, recall the myth of American achievement. Within his critique of American cultural practices, then, is an affirmation of its definitions of manhood and power.[16]

Frederick Douglass's *Narrative* participates in one of the major ideological controversies of his day, the dispute over the question of Negro humanity and equality. Rarely before the 1830s did slavery's apologists articulate a case for the innate inferiority of blacks. They argued instead that slavery was necessary not only to support the agrarian economy but also to socialize blacks out of a condition degraded by the circumstances of their environment. Only after the rise of the abolitionist campaign did they develop a systematic theory of racial inferiority that justified the institution of slavery.[17] For a slave simply to write the story of his or her own life represented an assault on this line of argument, since to make oneself the subject of a narrative presumes both the worth of that self and its interest for a reader.[18] The structures of Douglass's *Narrative* may be seen to address subtly the apologists' arguments. By using various clusters of imagery and an overarching pattern to unify his account, he discloses a complex, symbolic meaning of his life that further evinces his humanity.

Critics have discussed the ways in which images of animals, ships, and sails bestow thematic unity on the events in Douglass's narrative.[19] His use of blood as an image for the human spirit also binds various events to one another and connects him to the suffering of other slaves. Repeatedly Douglass asks the reader to visualize the blood that masters draw from their slaves. It is not enough to say that his Aunt Hester is beaten with a whip. Instead he writes that as a young child he watched his aunt being beaten with a "blood-clotted cowskin" where "the blood ran fastest," until she is "literally covered with blood" (p. 28). This experience marks Douglass's passage from the gate stained with his fellows' blood, from naiveté to understanding. Of Demby, a run-away slave shot by his own master, he writes: Demby's "mangled body sank out of sight and blood and brains marked the water where he had stood" (p. 47). To verify his assertion that self-professed Christians make the worst masters, he recalls an incident in which Captain Auld, his owner, whipped a lame young woman, "causing the warm red blood to drip" (p. 85). Passages such as these provide vivid symbols of the process of dehumanization that slaves underwent as their lifeblood was literally sapped. Significantly, after Douglass whips Covey and achieves the first stage of his ultimate emancipation, he underscores the fact that he himself lost not a drop of blood; on the contrary, he drew blood from the "nigger-breaker."

The primary figure for the meaning of Douglass's life is, however, a pattern that oscillates between slavehood and manhood. The rhetoric of the opening chapter demonstrates several of the ways in which the institution closes off the categories and relationships that ordinarily circumscribe human identity and thus dehumanizes slaves.[20] Douglass, for example, does not know his age and can say little about his parentage. Son of a black woman and her master, he possesses origins that offer counterevidence of his humanity, for his very existence derives from the conflation of sexual and property rights that slavery endorsed. His account, like those of so many of his counterparts, reminds us that by raping their women slaves, masters simultaneously obtained sexual satisfaction and increased their store of human property. Douglass is, therefore, to his master-father nothing more than "chattel personal," with no particular right to either a birth date or parental affection.

During his earliest years Douglass lived with other slave children in his grandmother's cottage on the outskirts of the plantation. As a result he remained ignorant of the brutalities of slavery until he was old enough to work. He dates his initiation into the meaning of his status from the time he watched his aunt being beaten for daring to visit her lover. Plummer, her master, strips her to the waist, crosses and ties her hands, and hangs her from a hook in a joist. He then beats her until her blood runs. As he watches this scene, the young Douglass is forced to confront the physical and emotional horror of slavery: "[It] was the blood-stained gate, the entrance to the hell of slavery, through which [he] was about to pass" (p. 28). Paradoxically, this recognition also makes possible his ultimate escape to freedom, because it compels him to acknowledge the horrors of his condition. On a profound level it thus initiates the process by which the slave was first "made a man" (p. 97).

Douglass's first stay in Baltimore is the culmination of this initial movement from slavehood to manhood, for in the city he learns to read and write. In this episode he creates what has become a prototypical situation for later Afro-American writers by linking the acquisition of literacy to both the act of rebellion and the achievement of freedom. As Albert E. Stone notes, Douglass sets up the journey in emblematic terms, foreshadowing its significance as a new stage in the development of his identity.[21] Before leaving for Baltimore he spends "three days in the creek, washing off the plantation scurf and preparing [himself] for his departure" (p. 52). En route to the city, he rides in the bow of the sloop, literally and figuratively "looking ahead" (p. 54).

Douglass begins to learn to read because his naive, originally well-intentioned mistress, Mrs. Auld, does not realize that as a slave, he is to be treated differently from a white child. Just as she discourages his "crouching servility" (p. 57) in her presence, so does she begin to teach him upon discovering his illiteracy. More sophisticated in the ways of the slave system than his wife is, Mr. Auld puts an abrupt end to

Douglass's education. But by revealing that literacy would "unfit him to be a slave" (p. 58), Auld kindles Douglass's nascent rebelliousness and yearning for freedom. Although the young slave does not yet understand the explicit connection between freedom and literacy, he is inspired to learn to read and write by any available means, precisely because his master denies him this privilege and associates these two forbidden fruits (that is, freedom and literacy) with each other. Douglass acknowledges that although he has lost his means of education, he has acquired an "invaluable instruction" about his condition from the very master who tries to keep him ignorant. As both Stone and Stephen Butterfield indicate,[22] Douglass's use of antithesis in this section of the *Narrative* reveals his budding awareness of the disjunction between his oppressor's interests and his own: "What [Auld] most dreaded, that I most desired. What he most loved, that I most hated. That which to him was a great evil, to be carefully shunned, was to me a great good, to be diligently sought; and the argument which he so warmly urged, against my learning to read, only served to inspire me with a desire and determination to learn" (p. 59).

The acquisition of literacy facilitates Douglass's achievement of freedom in two ways. The act of reading provides the intellectual basis of his quest for liberation, introducing him to forbidden and unfamiliar ideas such as freedom and abolition. Indeed, his new skill apprises him of so many notions that he comes to consider literacy a mixed blessing:

What I got from Sheridan was a bold denunciation of slavery, and a powerful vindication of human rights. *The reading of these documents* enabled me to utter my thoughts, and to meet the arguments brought forward to sustain slavery; but while they relieved me of one difficulty, they brought on another even more painful than the one of which I was relieved . . . In moments of agony, I envied my fellow slaves for their stupidity. (66–67; emphasis mine)

Learning to write, in contrast, enables him to manipulate the language of his superordinate to his own advantage. When he first attempts to escape, he writes passes or protections for himself and two fellow slaves. The narrative itself is, moreover, a symbolic, self-authored protection, for in the process of presenting and organizing his experiences, Douglass celebrates his achievement of autonomy.

After the independent-minded, newly literate Douglass returns to the plantation from Baltimore, his owner, Master Thomas, sends him to work for Covey, "the nigger-breaker." Because of Covey's persistent abuse, Douglass loses much of his independence of mind and slips back into the emotional lethargy he associates with mental and physical enslavement. But if the acquisition of literacy first enabled him to feel free, the act of physical resistance precipitates his second and lasting period of liberation. Indeed, if the sight of his aunt's wrongful punishment initiated him into slavery, one might argue that he emancipates himself by revising that earlier episode and refusing to be beaten:

This battle with Mr. Covey was the turning-point in my career as a slave. It rekindled the few expiring embers of freedom, and revived within me a sense of my own manhood. It recalled the departed self-confidence, and inspired me again with a determination to be free . . . My long-crushed spirit rose, cowardice departed, bold defiance took its place; and now I resolved that, however long I might remain a slave in form, the day had passed when I could be a slave in fact . . .

From this time I was never again what might be called

fairly whipped, though I remained a slave for four years afterwards. I had several fights but was never whipped.

(pp. 104–105)

Douglass's *Narrative* thus celebrates both explicitly and symbolically a slave's capacity to achieve humanity in a system that conspires to reduce him to nothing. In his ironies and diatribes alike, he exposes the fundamental contradictions of the slaveholding system that make a mockery of American principles and Christian mores. As I suggested earlier, he argues that the slavocracy potentially destroys the sanctity of family relations. Furthermore, his countless descriptions of the conditions under which slaves live rebut any theories that slaves love their assigned station or are humanized by the system. He discredits the apologists' evidence of the slaves' contentment by decoding the misery contained within their songs. And he reveals the misuses to which slaveholders put their religious beliefs. Indeed, in his description of the racism he confronts in New Bedford, he debunks even the myth of the North as a Promised Land.

By uncovering such systemic contradictions Douglass seems to call for a radical cultural transformation. Equiano had modified praise for slavery as an institution because it offered him opportunities to learn a skill, introduced him to Christianity, and provided him with the protection of kind masters. But Douglass's tone is sufficiently acerbic that even in his appendix, where he tries to clarify his position on Christianity, he fails to distinguish effectively his contempt for the slaveholder's religion from a general critique of religion.

And yet, as Houston A. Baker, Jr., and Annette Niemtzow have argued, Douglass is entrapped by the very rhetorical and ideological structures he seeks to undermine. Baker demonstrates that by associating freedom with a Christian context, Douglass displays his inability to imagine a self distinct from his superordinate's construction of identity.[23] Similarly, Niemtzow argues that merely by writing about himself in the form of autobiography, Douglass defines himself according to the values of the mainstream culture.[24] I would further suggest that the plot of the narrative offers a profound endorsement of the fundamental American plot, the myth of the self-made man. His broad-based indictments notwithstanding, by telling the story of one man's rise from slavery to the station of esteemed orator, writer, and statesman, he confirms the myth shared by generations of American men that inner resources alone can lead to success.

This myth ignores the role of historical forces in making some men more equal than others. By failing to acknowledge the impact of economic and political policy on individual circumstance, it denies the necessity of social reform to ensure genuine equality of opportunity. Douglass articulates numerous ways in which the slavocracy conspires against black achievement. Surely he believes that American society requires widespread transformation. But the story of his own success actually provides counterevidence for his platform of radical change; for by demonstrating that a slave can be a man in terms of all the qualities valued by his northern middle-class reader—physical power, perseverance, literacy—he lends credence to the patriarchal structure largely responsible for his oppression.

The details of Equiano's situation allow him a distance from Western ideology unavailable to Douglass. The alien origins of Equiano's discourse enable him to redefine the meaning of Christian conversion to suit his own purposes. Douglass, however, attempts to articulate a radical position using the discourse he shares with those against whom he speaks. What begins as an indictment of mainstream practice actually authenticates one of its fundamental assumptions. So if Douglass's own story supersedes the power of ancillary documents to verify his voice,[25] the meaning of his life is grounded in the very premises that contributed to his enslavement.[26]

Like that of her male counterparts, Harriet Jacobs's freedom to reconstruct her life was limited by a genre that suppressed subjective experience in favor of abolitionist polemics. But if slave narrators in general were restricted by the antislavery agenda, she was doubly bound by the form in which she wrote, for it contained a plot more compatible with received notions of masculinity than with those of womanhood. As Niemtzow has suggested, Jacobs incorporated the rhetoric of the sentimental novel into her account, at least in part because it provided her with a way of talking about her vulnerability to the constant threat of rape. This form imposed upon her restrictions of its own.[27] Yet she seized authority over her literary restraints in much the same way that she seized power in life. From within her ellipses and ironies—equivalents of the garret in which she concealed herself for seven years—she expresses the complexity of her experience as a black woman.

In *Incidents in the Life of a Slave Girl,* the account of her life as a slave and her escape to freedom, Harriet Jacobs refers to the crawl space in which she concealed herself for seven years as a "loophole of retreat."[28] The phrase calls attention both to the closeness of her hiding place—three feet high, nine feet long, and seven feet wide—and the passivity that even voluntary confinement imposes. For if the combined weight of racism and sexism have already placed inexorable restrictions upon her as a black female slave in the antebellum South, her options seem even narrower after she conceals herself in the garret, where just to speak to her loved ones jeopardizes her own and her family's welfare.

And yet Jacobs's phrase "the loophole of retreat" possesses an ambiguity of meaning that extends to the literal loophole as well. For if a loophole signifies for Jacobs a place of withdrawal, it signifies in common parlance an avenue of escape. Likewise, and perhaps more important, the garret, a place of confinement, also renders the narrator spiritually independent of her master, and makes possible her ultimate escape to freedom. It is thus hardly surprising that Jacobs finds her imprisonment, however uncomfortable, an improvement over her "lot as a slave" (p. 117). As her statement implies, she dates her emancipation from the time she entered her loophole, even though she did not cross into the free states until seven years later. Given the constraints that framed her life, even the act of choosing her own mode of confinement constitutes an exercise of will, an indirect assault against her master's domination.[29]

The plot of Jacobs's narrative, her journey from slavery to freedom, is punctuated by a series of similar structures of confinement, both literal and figurative. Not only does she spend much of her time in tiny rooms (her grandmother's garret, closets in the homes of two friends), but she seems as well to have been penned in by the importunities of Dr. Flint, her master: "My master met me at every turn, reminding me that I belonged to him, and swearing by heaven and earth that he would compel me to submit to him. If I went out for a breath of fresh air after a day of unwearied toil, his footsteps dogged me. If I knelt by my mother's grave, his dark shadow fell on me even there" (p. 27). Repeatedly she escapes overwhelming persecutions only by choosing her own space of confinement: the stigma of unwed motherhood over sexual submission to her master; concealment in one friend's home, another friend's closet, and her grandmother's garret over

her own and her children's enslavement on a plantation; Jim
Crowism and the threat of the Fugitive Slave Law in the
North over institutionalized slavery at home. Yet each moment of apparent enclosure actually empowers Jacobs to redi-
rect her own and her children's destiny. To borrow Elaine
Showalter's formulation, she inscribes a subversive plot of
empowerment beneath the more orthodox, public plot of
weakness and vulnerability.[30]

It is not surprising that both literal and figurative enclo-
sures proliferate in Jacobs's narrative. As a nineteenth-
century black woman, former slave, and writer, she labored
under myriad social and literary restrictions that shaped the
art she produced.[31] Feminist scholarship has shown that, in
general, women's writing in the nineteenth and twentieth
centuries has been strongly marked by imagery of confinement, a pattern of imagery that reflects the limited cultural options available to the authors because of their gender and chosen profession. Sandra Gilbert and Susan Gubar,
for instance, describe the prodigious restraints historically
imposed upon women that led to the recurrence of structures
of concealment and evasion in their literature.[32] Not only
were they denied access to the professions, civic responsibilities, and higher education, but also their secular and
religious instruction encouraged them from childhood to
adopt the "feminine," passive virtues of "submissiveness,
modesty, self-lessness."[33] Taken to its extreme, such an
idealization of female weakness and self-effacement contributed to what Ann Douglas has called a "domestication of
death," characterized by the prevalence in literature of a
hagiography of dying women and children, and the predilec-
tion in life for dietary, sartorial, and medical practices that led
to actual or illusory weakness and illness.[34]

Literary women confronted additional restraints, given the
widespread cultural identification of creativity with male-

ness. As Gubar argues elsewhere, our "culture is steeped in . . . myths of male primacy in theological, artistic, and scientific creativity," myths that present women as art objects, perhaps, but never as creators.[35] These ideological restraints, made concrete by inhospitable editors, publishers, and reviewers and disapproving relatives and friends have, as Gilbert and Gubar demonstrate, traditionally invaded women's literary undertakings with all manner of tensions. The most obvious sign of nineteenth-century women writers' anxiety about their vocation (but one that might also be attributed to the demands of the literary marketplace) is the frequency with which they published either anonymously or under a male pseudonym. Their sense of engaging in an improper enterprise is evidenced as well by their tendency both to disparage their own accomplishments in autobiographical remarks and to inscribe deprecations of women's creativity within their fictions. Moreover, they found themselves in a curious relation to the implements of their own craft. The literary conventions they received from genres dominated by male authors perpetuated reductive, destructive images of women that cried out to be revised. Yet the nature of women writers' socialization precluded their confronting problematic stereotypes directly. Instead, as Patricia Meyer Spacks, Carolyn Heilbrun, and Catharine Stimpson, as well as Showalter and Gilbert and Gubar have shown, the most significant women writers secreted revisions of received plots and assumptions either within or behind the more accessible content of their work.[36]

Jacobs's *Incidents* reveals just such a tension between the manifest and the concealed plot. Jacobs explicitly describes her escape as a progression from one small space to another. As if to underscore her helplessness and vulnerability, she indicates that although she ran alone to her first friend's home, she left each of her hiding places only with the aid of someone else. In fact, when she goes to her second and third hiding places, she is entirely at the mercy of her companion, for she is kept ignorant of her destination. Yet each closet, while at one level a prison, may be seen as well as a station on her journey to freedom. Moreover, from the garret of her seven-year imprisonment she uses to her advantage all the power of the voyeur—the person who sees but remains herself unseen. When she learns that Sands, her white lover and the father of her children, is about to leave town, she descends from her hiding place and, partly because she catches him unawares, is able to secure his promise to help free her children. In addition, she prevents her own capture not merely by remaining concealed but, more important, by embroiling her master, Dr. Flint, in an elaborate plot that deflects his attention. Fearing that he suspects her whereabouts, she writes him letters that she then has postmarked in Boston and New York to send him off in hot pursuit in the wrong direction. Despite her grandmother's trepidation, Jacobs clearly delights in exerting some influence over the man who has tried to control her.

Indeed, if the architectural close places are at once prisons and exits, then her relationship to Sands is both as well. She suggests that when she decides to take him as her lover, she is caught between Scylla and Charybdis. Forbidden to marry the free black man she loves, she knows that by becoming Sands's mistress she will compromise her virtue and reputation. But, she remarks, since her alternative is to yield to the master she loathes, she has no choice but to have sexual relations with Sands. As she writes: "It seems less degrading to give one's self, than to submit to compulsion. There is something akin to freedom in having a lover who has no control over you, except that which he gains by kindness and attachment" (p. 55).

One might argue that Jacobs's dilemma encapsulates the

slave woman's sexual victimization and vulnerability. I do not mean to impugn that reading, but I would suggest that her relationship with Sands provides her with a measure of power. Out of his consideration for her, he purchases her children and her brother from Flint. William, her brother, eventually escapes from slavery on his own, but Sands frees the children in accordance with their mother's wishes. In a system that allowed the buying and selling of people as if they were animals, Jacobs's influence was clearly minimal. Yet even at the moments when she seems most vulnerable, she exercises some degree of control.

As the examples of Equiano and Douglass reveal, the representative hero of the slave narrative, like the archetypal hero of the *Bildungsroman,* moves from the idyllic life of childhood ignorance in the country into a metaphoric wilderness, in this case the recognition of his status as a slave. His struggle for survival requires him to overcome numerous obstacles, but through his own talents (and some providential assistance) he finds the Promised Land of a responsible social position, a job, and a wife. The slave narrative typically extols the hero's stalwart individuality. And the narratives of male slaves often link the escape to freedom to the act of physically subduing the master. Douglass writes, for instance, that once he had overpowered the man whose job it was to break him, then he knew that he would soon be free.

Like the prototypical *Bildungsroman* plot, however, the plot of the slave narrative does not adequately accommodate differences in male and female development.[37] Jacobs's tale is not the classic story of the triumph of the individual will; rather it is more a story of a triumphant self-in-relation.[38] With the notable exception of the narrative of William and Ellen Craft, most of the narratives by men represent the life in slavery and the escape as essentially solitary journeys. This is not to suggest that male slaves were more isolated than their female counterparts, but it does suggest that they were attempting to prove their equality, their manhood, in terms acceptable to their white, middle-class readers.

Under different, equally restrictive injunctions, Jacobs readily acknowledges the support and assistance she received, as the description of her escape makes clear. Not only does she diminish her own role in her escape, but she is also quick to recognize the care and generosity of her family in the South and her friends in the North. The opening chapter of her account focuses not on the solitary "I" of so many narratives but on Jacobs's relatives. And she associates her desire for freedom with her desire to provide opportunities for her children.

By mythologizing rugged individuality, physical strength, and geographical mobility, the narratives enshrine cultural definitions of masculinity.[39] The plot of the standard narrative may thus be seen as not only the journey from slavery to freedom but also the journey from slavehood to manhood. Indeed, that rhetoric explicitly informs some of the best-known and most influential narratives. In the key scene in William Wells Brown's account, for example, a Quaker friend and supporter renames the protagonist, saying, "Since thee has got out of slavery, thee has become a man, and men always have two names."[40] Douglass also explicitly contrasts slavehood with manhood, for he argues that learning to read made him a man but being beaten made him a slave. Only by overpowering his overseer was he able to become a man— thus free—again.

Simply by underscoring her reliance on other people, Jacobs reveals another way in which the story of slavery and escape might be written. But in at least one place in the narrative she makes obvious her problematic relation to the rhetoric she uses. The fourth chapter, "The Slave Who Dared to Feel Like a Man," bears a title reminiscent of one of the most familiar lines from Douglass's 1845 *Narrative*. Here Jacobs links three anecdotes that illustrate the fact that independence of mind is incompatible with the demands of life as a slave. She begins with a scene in which her grandmother urges her family to content themselves with their lot as slaves; her son and grandchildren, however, cannot help resenting her admonitions. The chapter then centers on the story of her Uncle Ben, a slave who retaliates when his master tries to beat him and eventually escapes to the North.

The chapter title thus refers explicitly to Ben, the slave who, by defending himself, dares to feel like a man. And yet it might also refer to the other two stories included in the chapter. In the first, Jacobs's brother, William, refuses to capitulate to his master's authority. In the second, Jacobs describes her own earliest resolution to resist her master's advances. Although the situation does not yet require her to fight back, she does say that her young arm never felt half so strong. Like her uncle and brother, she determines to remain unconquered.

The chapter focuses on Ben's story, then, but it indicates also that his niece and nephew can resist authority. Its title might therefore refer to either of them as well. As Jacobs suggests by indirection, as long as the rhetoric of the genre identifies freedom and independence of thought with manhood, it lacks a category for describing the achievements of the tenacious black woman.

As L. Maria Child's introduction, Jacobs's own preface, and the numerous asides in the narrative make clear, Jacobs was writing for an audience of northern white women, a readership that by midcentury had grown increasingly leisured, middle class, and accustomed to the conventions of the novel of domestic sentiment. Under the auspices of Child, herself an editor and writer of sentimental fiction, Jacobs constructed the story of her life in terms that her

reader would find familiar. Certainly Jacobs's *Incidents* contains conventional apostrophes that call attention to the interests she shares with her readers. But as an additional strategy
for enlisting their sympathy, she couches her story in the
rhetoric and structures of popular fiction.

The details of the narrator's life that made her experience as
a slave more comfortable than most are precisely those that
render her story particularly amenable to the conventions and
assumptions of the sentimental novel. Like Douglass's, slave
narratives often begin with an absence, the narrator announc-
ing from the first that he has no idea where or when he was
born or who his parents were. But Jacobs was fortunate
enough to have been born into a stable family at once nuclear
and extended. Although both of her parents died young, she
nurtured vivid, pleasant memories of them. Moreover, she
remained close to her grandmother, an emancipated, self-
supporting, property-owning black woman, and to her un-
cles and aunts, until she escaped to the North.

Jacobs's class affiliation, and the fact that she was subjected
to relatively minor forms of abuse as a slave, enabled her to
locate a point of identification both with her readers and with
the protagonists of sentimental fiction. Like them, she as-
pired to chastity and piety as consummate feminine virtues
and hoped that marriage and family would be her earthly
reward. Her master, for some reason reluctant to force her to
submit sexually, harassed her, pleaded with her, and tried to
bribe her into capitulating in the manner of an importunate
suitor like Richardson's seducer. He tells her, for example,
that he would be within his rights to kill her or have her
imprisoned for resisting his advances, but he wishes to make
her happy and thus will be lenient toward her. She likens his
behavior to that of a jealous lover on one occasion when he
becomes violent with her son. And he repeatedly offers to
make a lady of her if she will grant him her favors, volunteer-

ing to set her up in a cottage of her own where she can raise her children.

By pointing up the similarities between her own story and those plots with which her readers would have been familiar, Jacobs could thus expect her readers to identify with her suffering. Moreover, this technique would enable them to appreciate the ways in which slavery converts into liabilities the very qualities of virtue and beauty that women were taught to cultivate. This tactic has serious limitations, however. As is always the case when one attempts to universalize a specific political point, Jacobs here trivializes the complexity of her situation when she likens it to a familiar paradigm. Like Richardson's Pamela, Jacobs is her pursuer's servant. But Pamela is free to escape, if she chooses, to the refuge of her parents' home, while as Dr. Flint's property, Jacobs has severely limited options. Moreover, Mr. B., in the terms the novel constructs, can redeem his importunities by marrying Pamela and elevating her and their progeny to his position. No such possibility exists for Jacobs and her master. Indeed, the system of slavery, conflating as it does the categories of property and sexual relationships, ensures that her posterity will become his material possessions.

For other reasons as well, the genre seems inappropriate for Jacobs's purposes. As the prefatory documents imply, Jacobs's readers were accustomed to a certain degree of propriety and circumlocution in fiction. In keeping with cultural injunctions against women's assertiveness and directness in speech, the literature they wrote and read tended to be "exercises in euphemism" that excluded certain subjects from the purview of fiction.[41] But Jacobs's purpose was to celebrate her freedom to express what she had undergone, and to engender additional abolitionist support. Child and Jacobs both recognized that Jacobs's story might well violate the rules of decorum in the genre. Their opening statements express the tension between the content of the narrative and the form in which it appears.

Child's introduction performs the function conventional to the slave narrative of establishing the narrator's veracity and the reliability of the account. What is unusual about her introduction, however, is the basis of her authenticating statement: she establishes her faith in Jacobs's story on the correctness and delicacy of the author's manner.

> The author of the following autobiography is personally known to me, and her conversation and manners inspire me with confidence. During the last seventeen years, she has lived the greater part of the time with a distinguished family in New York, and has so deported herself as to be highly esteemed by them. This fact is sufficient, without further credentials of her character. I believe those who know her will not be disposed to doubt her veracity, though some incidents in her story are more romantic than fiction.
>   (p. xi)

This paragraph attempts to equate contradictory notions; Child implies not only that Jacobs is both truthful and a model of decorous behavior but also that her propriety ensures her veracity. Child's assumption is troublesome, since ordinarily decorousness connotes the opposite of candor: one equates propriety not with openness but with concealment in the interest of taste.

Indeed, later in her introduction Child seems to recognize that an explicit political imperative may well be completely incompatible with bourgeois notions of propriety. While in the first paragraph she suggests that Jacobs's manner guarantees her veracity, by the last she has begun to ask if questions of delicacy have any place at all in discussions of human injustice. In the last paragraph, for example, she writes, "I am well aware that many will accuse me of indecorum for presenting these pages to the public." Here, rather than equating truthfulness with propriety, she acknowledges somewhat apologetically that candor about her chosen subject may well violate common rules of decorum. From this point she proceeds tactfully but firmly to dismantle the usefulness of delicacy as a category where subjects of urgency are concerned. She remarks, for instance, that "the experiences of this intelligent and much-injured woman belong to a class which some call delicate subjects, and others indelicate." By pointing to the fact that one might identify Jacobs's story as either delicate or its opposite, she acknowledges the superfluity of this particular label.

In the third and fourth sentences of this paragraph Child offers her most substantive critique of delicacy, for she suggests that it allows the reader an excuse for insensitivity and self-involvement. The third sentence reads as follows: "This peculiar phase of slavery has generally been kept veiled; but the public ought to be made acquainted with its monstrous features, and I willingly take the responsibility of presenting them with the veil withdrawn." Here she invokes and reverses the traditional symbol of feminine modesty. A veil (read: euphemism) is ordinarily understood to protect the wearer (read: reader) from the ravages of a threatening world. Child suggests, however, that a veil (or euphemism) may also work the other way, concealing the hideous countenance of truth from those who choose ignorance above discomfort.

In the fourth sentence she pursues further the implication that considerations of decorum may well excuse the reader's self-involvement. She writes, "I do this for the sake of my sisters in bondage, who are suffering wrongs so foul, that our ears are too delicate to listen to them." The structure of this sentence is especially revealing, for it provides a figure for the narcissism of which she implicitly accuses the reader. A sentence that begins, as Child's does, "I do this for the sake of my sisters in bondage, who are suffering wrongs so foul that . . ." would ordinarily conclude with some reference to the "sisters" or the wrongs they endure. We would thus expect the sentence to read something like: "I do this for the sake of my sisters in bondage, who are suffering wrongs so foul that they must soon take up arms against their master," or "that they no longer believe in a moral order." Instead, Child's sentence rather awkwardly imposes the reader in the precise grammatical location where the slave woman ought to be. This usurpation of linguistic space parallels the potential for narcissism of which Child suggests her reader is guilty.

Child, the editor, the voice of form and convention in the narrative—the one who revised, condensed, and ordered the manuscript and "pruned [its] excrescences" (p. xi)—thus prepares the reader for its straightforwardness. Jacobs, whose life provides the narrative subject, in apparent contradiction to Child calls attention in her preface to her book's silences. Rather conventionally she admits to concealing the names of places and people to protect those who aided in her escape. And, one might again be tempted to say conventionally, she apologizes for the inadequacy of her literary skills. But in fact, when Jacobs asserts that her narrative is no fiction, that her adventures may seem incredible but are nevertheless true, and that only experience can reveal the abomination of slavery, she underscores the inability of her form adequately to capture her experience.

Although Child and Jacobs are aware of the limitations of genre, the account often rings false. Characters speak like figures out of a romance. Moreover, the form allows Jacobs to talk about her sexual experiences only when they are the result of her victimization. She becomes curiously silent about the fact that her relationship with Sands continued even after Flint no longer seemed a threat.

Its ideological assumptions are the most serious problem the form presents. Jacobs invokes a plot initiated by Richardson's *Pamela*, and recapitulated in nineteenth-century American sentimental novels, in which a persistent male of elevated social rank seeks to seduce a woman of a lower class. Through her resistance and piety, she educates her would-be seducer into an awareness of his own depravity and his capacity for true, honorable love. In the manner of Pamela's Mr. B, the reformed villain rewards the heroine's virtue by marrying her.

As is true with popular literature generally, this paradigm affirms the dominant ideology, in this instance (as in Douglass's case) the power of patriarchy.[42] As Tania Modleski and Janice Radway have shown, the seduction plot typically represents pursuit or harassment as love, allowing the protagonist and reader alike to interpret the male's abusiveness as a sign of his inability to express his profound love for the heroine.[43] The problem is one that Ann Douglas attributes to sentimentalism as a mode of discourse, in that it never challenges fundamental assumptions and structures: "Sentimentalism is a complex phenomenon. It asserts that the values a society's activity denies are precisely the ones it cherishes; it attempts to deal with the phenomenon of cultural bifurcation by the manipulation of nostalgia. Sentimentalism provides a way to protest a power to which one has already in part capitulated."[44] Like Douglass, Jacobs does not intend to capitulate, especially since patriarchy is for her synonymous with slavocracy. But to invoke that plot is to invoke the clusters of associations and assumptions that surround it.

As Jacobs exercises authority over the limits of the male narrative, however, she triumphs as well over the limits of the sentimental novel, a genre more suited to the experience of her white, middle-class reader than to her own. From at least three narrative spaces, analogs to the garret in which she concealed herself, she displays her power over the forms at her disposal.

In a much-quoted line from the last paragraph of her account she writes: "Reader, my story ends with freedom, not in the usual way, with marriage" (p. 207). In this sentence she calls attention to the space between the traditional happy ending of the novel of domestic sentiment and the ending of her story. She acknowledges that however much her story may resemble superficially the story of the sentimental heroine, as a black woman she plays for different stakes; marriage is not the ultimate reward she seeks.

Another gap occurs at the point where she announces her second pregnancy. She describes her initial involvement with Sands as a conundrum. The brutality of neighboring masters, the indifference of the legal system, and her own master's harassment have forced her to take a white man as her lover. Both in the way she leads up to this revelation and in the apostrophes to the reader, she presents it as a situation in which she had no choice. Her explanation for taking Sands as her lover is accompanied by expressions of the appropriate regret and chagrin and then followed by two general chapters about slave religion and the local response to the Nat Turner rebellion. When we return to Jacobs's story, she remarks that Flint's harassment has persisted, and she announces her second pregnancy by saying simply, "When Dr. Flint learned that I was again to be a mother, he was exasperated beyond measure" (p. 79). Her continued relationship with Sands and her own response to her second pregnancy are submerged in the subtext of the two previous chapters and in the space between paragraphs. By consigning to the narrative silences those aspects of her own sexuality for which the genre does not allow, Jacobs points to an inadequacy in the form.

The third such gap occurs a bit later, just before she leaves the plantation. Her master's great aunt, Miss Fanny, a kind-hearted elderly woman who is a great favorite with Jacobs's grandmother, comes to visit. Jacobs is clearly fond of this woman, but as she tells the story, she admits that she resents Miss Fanny's attempts to sentimentalize her situation. As Jacobs tells it, Miss Fanny remarks at one point that she "wished that I and all my grandmother's family were at rest in our graves, for not until then should she feel any peace about us" (p. 91). Jacobs then reflects privately that "the good old soul did not dream that I was planning to bestow peace upon her, with regard to myself and my children; not by death, but by securing our freedom." Here, Jacobs resists becoming the object of someone else's sentimentality and calls attention to the inappropriateness of this response. Although she certainly draws on the conventions of sentimentalism when they suit her purposes, she is also capable of replacing the self-indulgent mythicization of death with the more practical solution of freedom.

The complex experience of the black woman has eluded analyses and theories that focus on any one of the variables of race, class, and gender alone. As Barbara Smith has remarked, the effect of the multiple oppression of race, class, and gender is not merely arithmetic.[45] That is, one cannot say only that in addition to racism, black women have had to confront the problem of sexism. Rather, issues of class and race alter one's experience of gender, just as gender alters the experience of class and race. Whatever the limitations of her narrative, Jacobs anticipates recent developments in class, race, and gender analysis. Her account indicates that this story of a black woman does not emerge from the superimposition of a slave narrative on a sentimental novel. Rather, in the ironies and silences and spaces of her book, she makes not quite adequate forms more truly her own.

TWO

Privilege and Evasion in The Autobiography of an Ex-Colored Man

As we have seen, the slave narrators illuminate the relationship between narrative authority and personal autonomy in the places in which they transform received literary and ideological conventions. By seizing control of the narrative representation of their lives, they provide a figure for their earlier escape from their masters' domination. In contrast, James Weldon Johnson's *The Autobiography of an Ex-Colored Man* (1912), a pivotal text in Afro-American letters, articulates by counterexample the relation between aesthetic and political control. A novel that foreshadows the tropes and the narrative situation of Ralph Ellison's *Invisible Man* and echoes and revises the structures not only of the former slaves' accounts but also of W. E. B. Du Bois's book *The Souls of Black Folk,* Johnson's text, like all of these works, engages the interconnections of racial history and conditions with the life history of the individual. By virtue of his class and complexion, however, Johnson's narrator is able to eschew the meaning, burden, and responsibilities of blackness and to live as if he were white. His decision to pass for a white man typifies the self-protectiveness that characterizes his behavior throughout the narrative. This refusal to explore and confront the full meaning of his identity, in turn, is embodied in the hiatuses, ellipses, and evasions that abound in his tale.

To put it another way, the ex-colored man appears to assume responsibility for articulating the meaning of his identity by undertaking the autobiographical enterprise. But the narrative's circumlocutions—which are, along with the ex-colored man's anonymity, its most salient features—undercut the process of self-individuation that characterizes the writing of autobiography. The ex-colored man thus sets up a narrative situation that makes possible the naming of the self, only to unname himself systematically and shirk the responsibility of identity and individuality.

Any consideration of Johnson's novel must address two related questions: first, what does it mean for a work of fiction to call itself an autobiography, and second, what are the connections between the simulated autobiography[1] and Johnson's actual autobiography, *Along This Way* (1933). By calling itself an autobiography either explicitly (as this work does) or implicitly (as do, for example, *The Adventures of Huckleberry Finn, Invisible Man,* and *Lolita*), a novel directs the reader's attention to the narrator and to the act of telling. The notion of autobiography assumes the existence of a person who really lived and whose experiences provide at least the framework of the narrative he or she consigns to print. A novel that calls itself an autobiography, then, creates the illusion that its protagonist exists or has existed in the world outside his or her literary production. By positing the narrator's authenticity, Johnson (like Twain, Ellison, and Nabokov, among others) by extension highlights the narrative process, prompting the reader to consider the ontological meaning of the act of telling, the ex-colored man's particular purpose for telling his own story, and the interconnections between the life described and the form through which it is communicated.

When Johnson characterizes his ex-colored man not only as a mulatto musician, factory worker, and successful businessman but also as a storyteller, he places him in the tradition of Afro-American autobiographers.[2] He aligns him with those earlier narrators whose stories testified to their achievement of freedom, and who defied domination, at least that of their masters. Like his literary forebears, the ex-colored man experienced the effects of racism; a child of Reconstruction, he has endured subtler, more pernicious forms of oppression than those his progenitors born in slavery faced. Yet the very stories that his story invokes—narratives of enslavement and freedom, of the relation of authorship to authority—provide a standard by which we may measure and understand the limits of the ex-colored man's character and voice. The slave narrators link their sense of humanity to the capacity for resistance and to the ability to describe their development of identity. Unlike the prototypical former slave autobiographer, however, the ex-colored man capitulates whenever obstacles confront him, choosing always material security and personal safety over more precious and elusive goals. This tendency leads to his ultimate renunciation of the possibility of living meaningfully as a black man. Paradoxically, then, by seeking to escape the constraints of his racial identity, he ultimately lives out the stereotype he intends to avoid. Choosing namelessness and succumbing to cowardice, he relegates himself to a less than full humanity and to an evasive narrative persona.

A simulated autobiography not only assumes the prior existence of the narrator but also suggests the identity of author and narrator. Several critics of the novel have thus based their interpretations on the notion that the ex-colored man's story only thinly veils Johnson's own life and opinions.[3] Certainly Johnson's characterization of the ex-colored man draws on his own experiences. Both Johnson and the ex-colored man find their first sight of Atlanta disappointing. Both travel because of the patronage of a wealthy, dissipated young white man. Author and narrator alike are multilingual, and both give up successful musical careers. But these superficial similarities conceal profound differences between the ex-colored man and Johnson's public persona. On the most obvious level, Johnson had no choice but to live his life as a black man. In addition, while the ex-colored man seems to be isolated throughout his life—cut off from black and white peers alike because of his skin color, orphaned in his adolescence, fearful that his racial identity will be discovered—Johnson enjoyed fruitful personal and professional collaborations and relationships among his friends and family in the black middle class. These significant dissimilarities militate against our assuming Johnson's identity with his narrator, and prompt us instead to maintain an ironic attitude toward the ex-colored man.[4]

In his landmark essay on the novel, Joseph T. Skerrett, Jr., suggests a way of reading the relationship between narrator and author that I have found useful.[5] He argues that the ex-colored man is based on the character of Johnson's long-time friend J. Douglass Wetmore (called "D." in *Along This Way*), a man who passed for white and whom Johnson portrays (knowingly or otherwise) as an alter ego. Close boyhood friends, the two men attended Atlanta University together for a time and shared a series of professional partnerships in their young adulthood. Despite their intimacy, Skerrett notes, Johnson, plagued with insecurities and self-doubts, envied D.'s self-assurance and adventurousness, "the way in which he could challenge life."[6]

D.'s independence of spirit culminated in his decision to shrug off the onus of blackness, to marry his white fiancée, and to pass for white. This choice, however, was unavailable to Johnson. Throughout his account he demonstrates the ef-

fects of changes in the racial and political climate on his personal experience. He thus makes clear that the fact and meaning of race were for him inescapable.

This is not to suggest that Johnson represents his blackness
as burdensome. Like many autobiographers (particularly
American autobiographers), Johnson argues that the dif-
ficulties he confronted (in his case the consequences of his
racial identity) were also the source of his creativity and
power. His experience as a rural summer-school teacher, for
instance, introduced him to the bleak economic and educational conditions under which blacks lived in the backwoods
of Georgia. Yet, as he puts it, his triumphs and failures alike
among the black poor figured centrally in the development of
his identity. Of this experience he writes:

> It was this period that marked the beginning of my psy-
> chological change from boyhood to manhood. It was this
> period that marked the beginning of my knowledge of my
> own people as a "race." That statement may not be en-
> tirely clear; I mean: I had in the main known my own
> people as individuals or as groups; and now I began to
> perceive them clearly as a classified division, a defined sec-
> tion of American society. I had learned something about
> the Negro as a problem, but now I was where I could
> touch the crude bulk of the problem itself with my own
> hands, where the relations between Black and White in the
> gross were pressed upon me.   (p. 119)

Furthermore, the insight and self-knowledge he derived
from his educational and antilynching work formed the cru-
cible for his most compelling and enduring poetry, "Lift
Ev'ry Voice and Sing" and *God's Trombones—Seven Negro
Sermons in Verse*.

A survey of Johnson's career and professional successes reveals the extent of his commitment to working for political change and racial uplift. Whether describing his work as teacher, principal, journalist, musician, novelist, poet, diplomat, civil rights leader, or university professor, he is careful to show the seriousness of his commitment to the imperatives he received from his formal and family education. Reflecting on his college years, he remarks:

> The conception of education then held at [Atlanta University] and at other Negro colleges belonged to an age that, probably, is passing never to return. The central idea embraced a term that is now almost a butt for laughter— "service." We were never allowed to entertain any thought of being educated as "go-getters." Most of us knew that we were being educated for life work as underpaid teachers. The ideal constantly held up to us was of education as a means of living, not of making a living. It was impressed upon us that taking a classical course would have an effect of making us better and nobler, and of higher value to those we should have to serve.   (p. 122)

Later the voice of conscience enables him to resist his brother's suggestion that he give up his principalship for a career in musical theater:

> [Rosamond's] enthusiasm roused my curiosity about this new world into which he had had a peep, and I became, as I had at times before and have many times since, keenly aware of the love of venture that runs in me, a deep, strong current. But I have from my father a something—which I have often thought limits me as an artist—that generally keeps that deep, strong current from bursting out and

spreading over the surface . . . I have often rebelled against these cautious admonitions; but, generally, I have followed them, saying to myself in justification: One need not be an irresponsible fool in order to be a good artist.   (p. 122)

This passage reveals a polarization within Johnson between the impulse toward duty and responsibility on the one hand and toward adventure on the other. The tone displays the fascination with nonconformity that figured in his reflections even near the end of his life. To some degree Johnson acted out this impulse: his eventual decision to leave Stanton High School, where he was principal, along with his subsequent career changes demonstrates that he may well have underestimated his own adventurousness. But despite these professional experiments, Johnson suggests throughout his autobiography that his choice of work and his ability to carry out his responsibilities were always affected by changes in the broad social condition of black Americans. I therefore believe that part of his fascination with D.—and, by extension, with the ex-colored man—was his curiosity about what it might mean to explore life's possibilities without these "cautious admonitions."

The simulated autobiography thus provided Johnson with an opportunity to explore a path he did not choose in life, but one that fascinated him nonetheless. If in life the fact and meaning of his race figured centrally in the development of his identity and provided him with a sense of mission, his novel enabled him to envisage what that life, free of the burdens of the past and of a sense of social commitment, might be. At some level, however, Johnson might be said to deny his narrator this choice as effectively as he denied it to himself in life, for he demonstrates that while the avoidance of race is in some ways liberating, it derives from a kind of cowardice and carries its own consequences. In the case of the ex-colored man, the decision to pass for white closes off a resource from which creative expression might have sprung.

۶۵

The opening of *The Autobiography of an Ex-Colored Man* recalls the beginning of many slave narratives. Comparison reveals salient features of the narrator's character and suggests the limits of his reliability. Born in a small southern town, he conceals the name of his place of birth and of his parents. Such silences often appear in slave narratives, but in the earlier texts they signify the narrators' ignorance of the details of their origins—one of the institutional abuses of slavery—or their need to protect either themselves or their friends and relatives. Born after the Civil War, and apparently with no black relatives still living, the ex-colored man fears neither recrimination under the slave codes nor recapture under the Fugitive Slave Law. Rather, his circumspection is prompted by the desire to protect his white relatives from embarrassment, and of course to protect his public identity as a white man.

Like many former slave narrators, the ex-colored man is the product of an alliance between a black woman and her white master-employer. This "slave family" proves to be as vulnerable to dissolution as were its prototypes, for the narrator and his mother are sent north to live apart from the white man who is both father and lover. The narrator's childhood journey to Connecticut may invite comparison with the ritual escape to the North; but I would argue that it recalls more closely those auctions, legion in the earlier texts, in which families are separated for the master's material and financial convenience. This is not to deny the fact that the move north opens up educational opportunities for the young mulatto boy. But the fact that after the separation his mother pines away for her lover reminds us that this gesture

differs qualitatively from the flight north to freedom under-
taken voluntarily.

Before sending away his son and his lover, the white master encircles the boy's neck with a gold coin on a string. The
gift confirms symbolically the limited freedom that derives
from the move north: "I remember how I sat upon his knee
and watched him laboriously drill a hole through a ten-dollar
gold piece, and then tie the coin around my neck with a
string. I have worn that gold piece around my neck the
greater part of my life, and still possess it, but more than once
I have wished that some other way had been found of attach-
ing it to me besides putting a hole through it."[7] This gesture
demonstrates the mother's and son's continued subordination to the white lover-father despite their geographical separation. The lover-father might be said to affix a financial
value to his son: the necklace functions as a yoke or restraint
by means of which he continues to exert his control. Oblivious to the meaning of the ritual, however, the narrator is
implicated in his own oppression, for he cherishes and yearns
to use the very coin by which his own value is determined.

The ex-colored man's revision of central tropes from the
narratives—the silences, the journey north, the auction—
exemplify the way he avoids engaging with the meaning of
his racial identity. He leaves undisturbed his present comfort
and security, glossing over the political implications of his
past circumstance. His choosing to live as a white man is thus
the culmination of a series of similar evasions.

Two experiences from his young adulthood typify his general refusal to confront psychological or economic discomfort. He arrives in Atlanta to attend the university, buoyed
up by his own expectations and the hopes of his neighbors
and his mother, now deceased. A self-described "perfect little
aristocrat" (p. 7), he finds the rusticity of the city and the
poverty of its black population repugnant, and is thus re-

lieved that Atlanta University, with its terraces, manicured lawns, and shady walks, seems remote from the squalor of the outside world. Because of his naiveté, however, the narrator promptly loses the money that was to have financed his education; thus in an instant he loses the distinction that money bestows and becomes indistinguishable from the people he had recently scorned. When he realizes his situation, he decides to seek the aid and advice of the university president. But, envisaging himself as the subordinate of someone he had formerly imagined to be his equal, he decides instead to quit school and seek his fortune elsewhere:

> As I neared the grounds, the thought came across me, would not my story sound fishy? Would it not place me in the position of an impostor or beggar? What right had I to worry these busy people with the results of my carelessness? If the money could not be recovered, and I doubted that it could, what good would it do to tell them about it? The shame and embarrassment which the whole situation gave me caused me to stop at the gate. I paused, undecided, for a moment; then turned and slowly retraced my steps, and so changed the whole course of my life. (p. 63)

The narrator's inability to conceive of the president as compassionate and generous derives from his own contempt for the impoverished and unfortunate. Obsessed by the need to operate from a position of power or privilege, he renounces the worthy goal of education rather than admit his distress. He perceives misfortune as a mark of shame, to be denied at all costs. It does not occur to him that adversity, inevitable in the life of the individual, may be overcome and may teach important lessons.

Similarly, the narrator abandons his first fiancée when his financial security is threatened. Granted, his relationship to her figures only marginally in his description of his life in Jacksonville, Johnson's own hometown and the place to which the narrator moves after he leaves Atlanta. He provides in the Jacksonville chapter a detailed description of his work in the cigar factory and a close analysis of the class system within which southern blacks operate; he mentions his engagement to the young teacher only to indicate how pleasant and comfortable his life in Florida is. Nevertheless, when the cigar factory closes unexpectedly, he appears never even to think about finding other work or marrying despite the setback. He runs from this misfortune as easily as he had left Atlanta behind:

> Just when I was beginning to look upon Jacksonville as my permanent home and was beginning to plan about marrying the young schoolteacher, raising a family, and working in a cigar factory the rest of my life, for some reason, which I do not remember, the factory at which I worked was indefinitely shut down. Some of the men got work in other factories in town; some decided to go to Key West and Tampa, others made up their minds to go to New York for work. All at once a desire like a fever seized me to see the North again and I cast my lot with those bound for New York. (p. 88)

The habitual evasiveness that influences the ex-colored man's decisions in life is evident also in the linguistic choices he makes as narrator. Throughout his account he resorts to circumlocutions whenever he must describe an experience that he considers painful. As early as the first two paragraphs of the novel, when he first approaches the issue of passing for white, he equivocates about his motives for telling his story. The abrupt shifts of tone in this opening section foreshadow his characteristic inability to confront, to interpret, and to learn from painful experiences:

> I know that in writing the following pages I am divulging the great secret of my life, the secret which for some years I have guarded far more carefully than any of my earthly possessions; and it is a curious study to me to analyze the motives which prompt me to do it. I feel that I am led by the same impulse which forces the unfound-out criminal to take somebody into his confidence, although he knows that the act is likely, even almost certain to lead to his undoing. I know that I am playing with fire, and I feel the thrill which accompanies that most fascinating pastime; and, back of it all, I think I find a sort of savage and diabolical desire to gather up all the little tragedies of my life, and turn them into a practical joke on society.
>
> And, too, I suffer a vague feeling of unsatisfaction, of regret, of almost remorse, from which I am seeking relief, and of which I shall speak in the last paragraph of this account. (p. 3)

In the first paragraph the narrator offers three reasons for telling his story. First, like an uncaptured criminal he enjoys flaunting his capacity to outwit his fellow man. Second, like a child he finds toying with danger titillating. And third, like a confidence man he delights in the trick he has played on society. He sets up the second paragraph to explain his final, most profound reason for writing the autobiography: in the process of narrating his story he hopes to exorcise his feelings of guilt. This paragraph, the second and more significant, is written with greater tentativeness and hesitation. He presents his superficial reasons with precision, likening himself to a criminal, a child, and a trickster to clarify his motives. But in the second paragraph he avoids exposing or confronting his deeper motives by retreating into the rhetoric of a single vague and convoluted sentence. Indeed, he delays discussing the direct object of his sentence—that is, what he "suffers from"—until the last paragraph of the novel.

The ex-colored man's childhood discovery that he is black constitutes one of the more traumatic moments of his life. His inability as a child to absorb the impact of that disclosure may well explain his difficulty in writing about it as an adult. Like Du Bois, the narrator discovers he is black while he is at school. Stunned by the revelation, he withdraws into himself, refusing to respond to his teacher and fellow students. At home later the same day he examines his face in the mirror as if for the first time. In his description of the episode he suggests that only when he looks at his reflection does he fully accept his blackness. The structure of the following paragraph reveals the narrator's attempt to set up this moment of self-recognition in emblematic terms. Having heard the truth about his origins, it suggests, he can see himself as he really is. In fact, his self-description only confirms his sense of his own whiteness; he sees only his white features, acknowledging none that might accurately indicate the other half of his racial heritage. The truth notwithstanding, he presents himself only as he wishes to be seen:

> For an instant I was afraid to look, but when I did, I looked long and earnestly. I had often heard people say to my mother: "What a pretty boy you have!" I was accustomed to hear remarks about my beauty; but now, for the first time, I became conscious of it and recognized it. *I noticed the ivory whiteness of my skin,* the beauty of my mouth, the size and liquid darkness of my eyes, and how the long, black lashes that fringed and shaded them produced an effect that was strangely fascinating even to me. *I noticed*

the softness and glossiness of my dark hair that fell in waves over my temples, making my forehead appear whiter than it really was.   (p. 17; emphasis mine)

This failure to see his color in the mirror symbolizes his characteristic inability to accept his racial identity. From the self-awareness of maturity, he might have remarked on this childhood defensiveness. That he neither corrects nor comments on this self-protectiveness as an adult indicates the ex-colored man's failure to move beyond it.

The young boy's subsequent response to this discovery further reveals his ambivalence and discomfort. On the one hand he demonstrates his curiosity about his race by committing himself to the research and study of black historical achievements. Yet on the other, by isolating himself from his black and white peers alike, he denies himself the full experience of his newly acknowledged identity. His descriptions from the point of view of an adult possess the same quality of distance. When he analyzes what the discovery of his blackness means, his language directly imitates Du Bois's language in the first chapter of *The Souls of Black Folk*. Faced with the complexity of his own experience, he adopts another writer's formulation.

He begins his exposition of his feelings in this section of the novel by searching for a metaphor he considers appropriate. Discovering that he is black is, he says, like his "first spanking." Like many "trivial incidents of childhood—a broken toy, a promise made to us which was not kept, a harsh, heart-piercing word," it retains even to his adult perspective the profound pain of "the tragedies of life" (p. 20). His explanation is troublesome for two reasons. First, by comparing the awakening of his racial consciousness to the disappointments of childhood, the narrator minimizes the significance of his experience. Second, his metaphor obscures rather than clarifies his meaning. By concentrating on what this revelation is *like,* the narrator avoids telling us what it *is.*

Relinquishing the search for an image, the ex-colored man proceeds to imitate, whether consciously or unconsciously, the resonances and language of the often-quoted first chapter of Du Bois's *The Souls.* The ex-colored man writes, "From that time *I looked out through other eyes,* my thoughts were colored, my actions limited by one dominating, all-pervading idea which constantly increased in force and weight until I finally realized in it a great, tangible fact" (p. 21; emphasis mine). His language echoes that of the following passage from *The Souls,* which similarly focuses on the tension between the way the white and black worlds look upon each other: "It is a peculiar sensation, this double-consciousness, this sense of always *looking at one's self through the eyes of others,* of measuring one's soul by the tape of a world that looks on in amused contempt and pity."[8] As Stepto demonstrates, the ex-colored man's transcription of the earlier text differs just enough from it to indicate that he has misread it.[9] But we should also note that this muddle occurs at the point at which he should be explaining the implications of what it means to be black. He can express his self-loathing only by filtering it through a faulty explication of a secondary text.

This same self-protectiveness later obscures the logical implications of his broader cultural analyses. For instance, he denies that a sense of inferiority prompts dark-skinned blacks to marry those fairer than themselves:

[Black] men generally marry women fairer than themselves; while on the other hand, the dark women of stronger mental endowment are very often married to light-complexioned men; the effect is a tendency toward lighter complexions, especially among the more active elements in the race. Some might claim that this is a tacit admission of coloured people among themselves of their own inferiority judged by the colour line. I do not think so. What I have termed an inconsistency is, after all, most natural; it is, in fact, a tendency in accordance with what might be called an economic necessity. So far as racial differences go, the United States put a greater premium on colour, or, better, lack of colour, than upon anything else in the world . . . It is this tremendous pressure which the sentiment of the country exerts that is operating on the race. (pp. 154–155)

This interpretation rests on the distinction he draws between black people's sense of inferiority and the "economic necessity" of color consciousness. He argues that blacks select in favor of fairer complexions because of the imperatives of the society they inhabit, not because they themselves believe in the superiority of whiteness. Certainly the two reasons need not exclude each other; the narrator could easily have considered both possibilities. But by underscoring only the social causes of this phenomenon, he ignores the self-loathing implicit in, and the politics of, such choices. The narrator here oversimplifies a complicated situation instead of confronting its unflattering implications.

The ex-colored man's lapses in logic, in interpretation, and in clarity are not the result of limited analytic abilities. Throughout the novel he lucidly considers the new places and kinds of people he encounters. He provides the reader with informed perspectives on Cuban workmen in a cigar factory, the black sporting life in New York, the uniqueness of black culture in Washington, D.C., the talents of the black preacher. He differentiates perspicaciously among the relationships that blacks in the "desperate class" (p. 76), the domestic class, and the independent class sustain with whites:

[Those in the "desperate class"] cherish a sullen hatred for all white men, and they value life as cheap. I have heard more than one of them say: "I'll go to hell for the first white man that bothers me . . ." [To the domestic class any] white person is "good" who treats them kindly, and they love him for that kindness. In return, the white people with whom they have to do regard them with indulgent affection . . . [Those in the independent class] live in a little world of their own . . . The proudest and fairest lady in the South could with propriety . . . go to the cabin of Aunt Mary her cook, . . . but if Mary's daughter, Eliza, a girl who used to run around my lady's kitchen, but who has received an education and married a prosperous young colored man, were at death's door, my lady would no more think of crossing the threshold of Eliza's cottage than she would of going into a bar-room for a drink.   (pp. 77–79)

He appreciates and describes the complex responsibilities of the improvisational music leader in the black church: "It is indispensable to the success of the singing, when the congregation is a large one made up of people from different communities, to have someone with a strong voice who knows just what hymn to sing and when to sing it, who can pitch it in the right key, and who has all the leading lines committed to memory" (p. 178). And he can analyze the harmony in congregational singing: "Generally the parts taken up by the congregation are sung in a three-part harmony, the women singing the soprano and a transposed tenor, the men with high voices singing the melody, and those with low voices a thundering bass. In a few of these songs, however, the leading part is sung in unison by the whole congregation, down to the last line, which is harmonized" (p. 180). In short, as long as the ex-colored man can remain at a distance from what he describes, he can articulate it clearly. Once his analyses impinge on his own relation to his racial identity, however, he is unable to sustain his acuity.

It is not surprising that the ex-colored man has difficulty confronting racial tension, since the society in which he comes of age is fractured by what Du Bois calls "the problem of the color line."[10] But he seems as well to share his mother's timidity and inability to face the truth. She never admits to her son (or, in his telling, he can never allow her to utter the words) that the two of them are black. When the ex-colored man asks if he is a "nigger," she "[hides] her face in [his] hair" and says, "No, my darling, you are not a nigger."

> "You are as good as anybody; if anyone calls you a nigger, don't notice them" . . . I stopped her by asking: "Well, am I white? Are you white?" She answered tremblingly: "No, I am not white, but you—your father is one of the greatest men in the country—the best blood of the South is in you—" . . . I almost fiercely demanded: "Who is my father? Where is he?" She stroked my hair and said: "I'll tell you about him some day." I sobbed: "I want to know now." She answered: "No, not now." (pp. 18–19)

As evasive as the son, the mother will neither lie nor speak the truth. And with comparable ambiguity, in the sentence that follows this paragraph the son punishes his mother for her indecisiveness: "Perhaps it had to be done, but I have never forgiven the woman who did it so cruelly" (p. 19). The next sentence clarifies for the reader that the woman to whom the ex-colored man refers is actually his teacher. But before we reach that sentence, we notice only that the antecedent of "the woman" is "she," his mother. Subconsciously the ex-colored man blames his mother for his disillusionment. Characteristically, his method of reconciling himself to an unpleasant situation—in this case accepting both his blackness and his anger at his mother—is to avoid it and fault someone else.

In the climactic episode of the novel, the narrator watches a black man being burned alive. He describes the spectacle in vivid detail:

> There he stood, a man only in form and stature, every sign of degeneracy stamped upon his countenance. His eyes were dull and vacant, indicating not a single ray of thought. Evidently the realization of his fearful fate had robbed him of whatever reasoning power he had ever possessed. He was too stunned and stupefied even to tremble. Fuel was brought from everywhere, oil, the torch, the flames crouched for an instant as though to gather strength, then leaped up as high as their victim's head. He squirmed, he writhed, strained at his chains, then gave out cries and groans that I shall always hear. The cries and groans were choked off by the fire and smoke; but his eyes, bulging from their sockets, rolled from side to side, appealing in vain for help. Some of the crowd yelled and cheered, others seemed appalled at what they had done, and there were those who turned away sickened at the sight. I was fixed to the spot where I stood, powerless to take my eyes from what I did not want to see.
>
> (pp. 186–187)

This scene dramatizes for him the extent of black oppression. While formerly he had tried to avoid seeing and identifying himself with both the victims and the perpetrators of such acts of injustice, on this occasion he cannot escape.

The sight of this lynching awakens feelings of shame, much like those he experienced after being robbed: It "was not discouragement or fear or search for a larger field of action and opportunity that was driving me out of the Negro race. I knew that it was shame, unbearable shame. Shame at being identified with a people that could with impunity be treated worse than animals" (pp. 190–191). As he turned his back on that earlier experience of psychic pain, here too he runs from this sense of shame. Instead of allowing the possibility of growth through suffering, he chooses to avoid it. He relinquishes his racial heritage altogether and reenters the world as a white man.

Like a number of his earlier choices, the narrator's decision to pass for white clearly allows him certain material and creature comforts. Leading a life unrestrained by political responsibilities or racial injustice, he is free to love the woman of his choice and to make a successful career in business and real estate. But the images with which the narrative ends reveal that by denying his past—both individual and racial—and his identity, the ex-colored man has also cut off the source of his creativity.[11] The choice to live as a white man may bring him economic stability, but all that remains of his talent is "a little box [of] . . . fast yellowing manuscripts, the only tangible remnants of a vanished dream, a dead ambition, a sacrificed talent" (p. 211).

Insofar as the ex-colored man operates as Johnson's alter ego, his fate may be seen to justify Johnson's own choices. Whatever discomforts his political work and public service may have caused him, Johnson seems to have believed that they became part of the fabric of his life and provided the source of his musical and literary productions. The narrator, by contrast, denies his race, a choice that, by extension, becomes linked inextricably to his artistic failure. Indeed the closing remarks about the "yellowing" musical compositions may well comment on the status of the novel as text and as autobiography. Surely if the ex-colored man's potential as a musician is compromised by his personal choices, then the quality of his narrative suffers as a result of his limited capacity for self-scrutiny.

The limits of the ex-colored man's autobiography therefore reflect his temperamental shortcomings. He never acquires verbal control over his experience because he cannot manage to look at his life with the necessary steadiness. The example of the slave narrators shows us that in the capacity to create a self in language lies autonomy. Our first modern case shows us that in the inability to articulate experience lies defeat.

THREE

ð

Alienation and Creativity in the Fiction of Richard Wright

As the examples of Equiano, Douglass, and Jacobs indicate, the slave narrators operated under a multiple burden. On the one hand, the politics of their situation as writers required them to point up the representative quality of their stories: it was incumbent upon them to sustain the illusion that their suffering typified the broader slave experience. On the other hand, as autobiographers and literate survivors of an oppressive system, they occupied a position that advertised their individuality. At one level they hoped to prove their common humanity with the readership to which their narratives were addressed. Yet at another they felt the need to distinguish themselves from the conceptions of humanness that were implicated in their oppression. Their texts thus work at cross-purposes, presenting the narrator-protagonists as simultaneously collective and unique personalities, at once similar to and different from their readers.

The situation of Johnson's ex-colored man, shot through with ambiguities as it is, recapitulates the double role of the slave narrator at a higher level of intensity. Both black and white, confessor and concealer, named and unnamed, real and imaginary, Johnson's narrator traverses in several ways the line that separates insider from outsider. Certainly his ambiguous racial identity works to his advantage as narrator: it enables him to write from the vantage point of both spectator at and participant in the worlds on both sides of the color line. Moreover, his persistent allusions to *The Souls of Black Folk* as subtext, and his problematic relation to the act of disclosure, provide emblems of his indeterminate status, a condition he shares with other black narrators, if not other blacks generally. Du Bois's oft-quoted formulation suggests, of course, that blacks in this culture are at once American and "other"; the ex-colored man demonstrates how his socialization and psychology lead him to feel simultaneously black and white.

Richard Wright, whose most acclaimed novel appeared over thirty years after Johnson's *Ex-Colored Man,* built a career around telling the story of the black outsider, a persona that his autobiography and biography suggest may well have arisen from his own experience. In *Black Boy* (1945), the first volume of his autobiography, he describes ways in which the black family, operating as an agent of the majority white culture, suppresses all signs of individuality and power in its youth in order to fit them for their subordinate position in the Jim Crow system. Willful, perceptive, and creative, young Richard refuses to internalize the restrictions of either his black or his white oppressors. His autobiographical protagonist is thus perpetually isolated within or moving beyond a restrictive community: the family, the black church, the South, the Communist party.[1]

As Katherine Fishburn's argument and methodology suggest, Wright's autobiography provides the ur-plot and protagonist for much of his fiction, even though it was written after *Lawd Today* (written in 1938 but not published until 1963), *Uncle Tom's Children* (1938), and *Native Son* (1940).[2] All of his protagonists occupy worlds closely circumscribed by racial and economic oppression. Even those few texts that open in comparatively idyllic, tranquil settings—"Big Boy Leaves Home" and "Long Black Song" (both in *Uncle Tom's Children*) and *The Long Dream* (1958)—foreshadow the characters' and the stories' unfortunate endings. The suspense that derives from the relentless plottedness (the area in which Wright's technical skill is perhaps most consistently demonstrated) symbolizes the nature of the oppression with which Afro-Americans live. This technique bespeaks a world devoid of options, where one's words and actions are closely scrutinized, and where one feels that the future has been scripted by some "other."

With the possible exception of Jake Jackson, the main character in *Lawd Today,* Wright's protagonists protect themselves from the tyranny of their oppressors by drawing on their resilience, imagination, and perceptiveness, qualities that make them, to Wright's mind, a threat to blacks and whites alike.[3] Two of the protagonists in *Uncle Tom's Children* (Mann in "Down by the Riverside" and Silas in "Long Black Song") suffer as a direct result of white oppression and the inadequacies of their own people. The central characters of "The Man Who Was Almost a Man" and "The Man Who Lived Underground"—both stories in *Eight Men* (published in 1960 but written from 1937 to 1957)—discover that they can live fully only when they escape their repressive communities of origin.

Cross Damon, the protagonist of *The Outsider* (1953), clearly invites comparison with the autobiographical persona; although not a writer himself, he alone among the protagonists shares young Richard's love of literature. Cross too feels entrapped within a black community he perceives as unsupportive, one whose limitations are symbolized by his problematic relations with the three black women in his life: his wife, mother, and lover. His reflections reveal his dislocated self-perception; he thinks of himself as, for example, "an absent man who was well known to him" and as someone whose problem is with "the relationship of himself to himself."[4] Likewise, as he and his friends recall, he has always seemed detached from other people, possessed by delusions of being a god, manipulating others rather than participating fully with them.

A train wreck grants him the opportunity to create himself anew. When he discovers that the world believes him to be dead, he takes on a new name, moves to New York, and leaves behind all of his confining associations. The novel demonstrates, however, that the past and future are linked inextricably; one cannot escape history simply by choosing a new beginning. Given a clean slate, Cross (now known as Lionel Lane) is drawn again into a complex of relations with Communist party members and with a woman he comes to love. Now a man with only a history of his own creation, he uses his freedom to execute anyone whose existence threatens him. But while he had originally thought that he yearned for isolation, he discovers that his humanity is embedded deeply in communal relations. His real search has been for connections through which he can be understood and accepted. As he remarks on his deathbed: "The search can't be done alone . . . Alone a man is nothing . . . Man is a promise that he must never break . . . I wish I had some way to give the meaning of my life to others . . . To make a bridge from man to man . . . Starting from scratch every time is . . . no good."[5]

The Long Dream, narrower in focus than either the naturalistic *Native Son* or the existential *Outsider,* explores with greater complexity the communal and familial dynamics that informed the training of southern black youth in the first half of this century.[6] Narrated as a series of vignettes from the childhood and youth of its protagonist, Fishbelly Tucker, the novel demonstrates the profound connections between the development of gender and racial identity. Like other male characters in the Wright corpus, Fishbelly finds the socialization process limiting. He too is especially alienated from black women. But the depth of his characterization allows him to express more ambivalence toward the forms of black male power than his precursors do. He is certainly contemptuous of the methods his father employs to remain in the good graces of the white establishment. But his sense of identity is implicated in his need to believe in, protect, and perpetuate the myth of his father's authority. It is thus only after his father's death and his own imprisonment (his atonement for his father's sins) that he escapes. Like Wright's other protagonists, he also seeks a new beginning in a world where he can live more fully.

By focusing his narratives on characters he believes to be exceptional, Wright portrays with contempt the larger black community, identifying it with what he sees as an extreme tendency toward accommodation.[7] Wright is especially judgmental with regard to black women, since his plots tend to recapitulate the cultural association of women with domesticity and socialization. Because to him these two impulses are implicated in the black man's oppression, his protagonists routinely reject their connections to black women as a stage in their search for liberation.[8] And yet, as my comments about *The Outsider* have suggested and my readings of the autobiographies and of *Native Son* will further indicate, the movement away from community in Wright's work is always accompanied by a search for newer, more fulfilling associations.

Ralph Ellison differentiates Bigger Thomas from the young Richard on the basis of their relative degrees of literacy and creativity.[9] But this is to define literacy and creativity too narrowly, thereby denying the fundamental similarities between the two characters. Not only do both Bigger and Wright rebel against the strictures of black and white authority, but both also rely on their ability to manipulate language and its assumptions—to tell their own stories—as a means of liberating themselves from the plots others impose on them. Moreover, each man seeks to alter his relation to language in order to break down the barriers that separate him from the broader social community.

≈❧

Near the beginning of *Black Boy* Wright describes a time when he tested the limits of his father's authority. His father, for whom the young Richard felt little more than contempt, worked as a night porter in a Memphis drugstore and needed quiet during the daytime in order to sleep. On one occasion Richard and his brother find a stray cat and begin to play with it in the apartment. The cat starts to meow loudly and persistently, and the boys can neither quiet the cat nor put it out.

As young Richard and his brother fear, the noise awakens their father, who orders them to get rid of the cat. When the boys' efforts fail, the father himself tries to drive it out, but still it remains. Finally, in exasperation the father yells, "*Kill that damn thing! . . . Do anything,* but get it away from here!"[10]

Resenting his father's anger, the young Richard retaliates by taking the command literally. Despite his brother's warning, Richard hangs the kitten. Characteristically, the younger brother tells their mother what Richard has done, and she punishes and frightens him by forcing him to untie and bury the cat and then pray to God for forgiveness. Before submitting Richard to this ordeal, his mother reports Richard's behavior to his father, and the following exchange ensues:

"You know better than that!" my father stormed.
"You told me to kill 'im," I said.

"I told you to drive him away," he said.

"You told me to kill 'im," I countered positively.

"You get out of my eyes before I smack you down!" my father bellowed in disgust, then turned over in bed.

I had had my first triumph over my father. I had made him believe that I had taken his words literally. He could not punish me now without risking his authority. I was happy because I had at last found a way to throw my criticism of him into his face. I had made him feel that, if he whipped me for killing the kitten, I would never give serious weight to his words again. I had made him know that I felt he was cruel and I had done it without his punishing me. (p. 11)

This scene is a crucial and prototypical one in this story of the writer's development, for it reveals to the young boy the power of language. Even at the age of five, he knows how to manipulate language and meaning to exercise control over his father. The young Richard knows that when his father tells him to kill the cat, he is speaking sarcastically. Yet Richard refuses to share his father's assumptions about what his words mean. Instead he takes the words literally. He asserts his own interpretation over and against his father's, thereby challenging his authority. The repetitions in the exchange between father and son reveal Richard's delight at the power the victory has given him. He has made his father believe that he has taken his words literally. He has made him see that if he were to be whipped for killing the kitten, he would never give serious weight to his father's words again. And he has made him know that he feels his father is cruel but has done so without being punished.

Ironically, Richard's mother regains authority over him by making him say words that frighten him. She requires him to repeat a prayer after her: "Dear God our Father, Forgive me for I knew not what I was doing. And spare my poor life, even though I did not spare the life of the kitten. And while I sleep tonight, do not snatch the breath of life from me" (p. 12). Richard cannot say the last line, because it evokes a terrifying image. As the narrator remarks: "I opened my mouth but no words came. My mind was frozen with horror. I pictured myself gasping for breath and dying in my sleep. I broke away from my mother and ran into the night, crying, and sharing my dread" (pp. 12–13).

In this incident Richard intentionally misconstrues his father's words; the consequences of his gesture of defiance far outweigh his expectations. Indeed, the autobiography is replete with episodes that remind Richard that his misappropriation of language has dramatic consequences. He does not intend, for example, to insult his grandmother or his uncle when he asks the one to kiss him "back there" (p. 36) and answers the other in an offhand manner. But because both remarks offend, the two episodes end violently.

When Richard finds himself at cross-purposes with whites, the consequences are graver still. In one instance he is almost killed when he forgets to call a white man "sir." Yet not all of the lessons he learns about the power of language are negative. He pretends to resent the attention he attracts when he publishes his first short story, "The Voodoo of Hell's Half-Acre." The remarks of his family and neighbors are strikingly inappropriate: no one understands why he would make up a story, why he would write it down, why he would have it published, why he would use the word *hell* in the title. Wright comments that such responses make him wish he had never written the story; but the reader remains unconvinced, for young Richard is clearly delighted to be published and to be the center of any attention, however misguided. Moreover, his achievement allows him to feel superior to his illiterate friends and relatives. His talent enables him to condescend to those people who try to diminish him.

Richard moves to Chicago in the hope of being able to develop his writing ability. The more he writes, the more convinced he becomes of his capacity to harness the power of language and turn it to his advantage. He comments in *American Hunger* that he hoped to learn to write with such precision that his readers would forget that they were reading, and would be caught up by the power of the emotion he described:

My purpose was to capture a physical state or movement that carried a strong subjective impression, an accomplishment which seemed supremely worth struggling for. If I could fasten the mind of the reader upon words so firmly that he would forget words and be conscious only of his response, I felt that I would be in sight of knowing how to write narrative. I strove to master words, to make them disappear, to make them important by making them new, to make them melt into a rising spiral of emotional stimuli, each greater than the other, each feeding and reinforcing the other, and all ending in an emotional climax that would drench the reader with a sense of a new world. That was the single aim of my living.[11]

Richard's rhetoric here recalls the kitten episode. Again he becomes enraptured by the possibility of obliterating the line between language and consciousness, and believes that his words will enable him to change the way people feel and think.

By the time he is ousted from the Communist party, however, Richard realizes that his very emotional survival may depend on his writing. Throughout his life he has felt like an outsider within his family, among his peers, and in white society. Being cast out of the party reaffirms this sense of alienation; he is now thoroughly convinced that he will never find a place where he is accepted for the complex person that he is. At the end of *American Hunger* he embraces his writing ability as the only way he can communicate with others. He has come to believe that only when he can get people to read his work will he finally be able to express individual and collective emotions, expressions to which his friends, family, and associates have always turned a deaf ear.

Writing his autobiography thus enabled Wright to address the problem of isolation in two ways. For him, as for most autobiographers, writing his own story provided a way of discovering or creating the essential unity of his life. By imposing narrative form on his lived experience, he converted the randomness of real events into the coherence of art. For Wright, as for the slave narrators before him, this process was particularly critical since he came of age in a world that aggressively denied his individuality. Writing his autobiography allowed him to challenge the docile, compliant identity—the inappropriate script—that others had tried to impose on him. By fashioning himself in language, he proved to his reader that he was unique, and that a specific set of forces and experiences combined to make him who he was.

Moreover, writing his autobiography helped Wright solve the problem of his isolation because it allowed him to establish contact with other people. He wanted, he said, to write with such precision that people would forget that they were reading. He believed that if he could get his readers to feel what he had felt at various periods in his life, then he would have established an intimacy that he was never able to attain in reality.

ॐ

As my earlier remarks suggest, the criticism of Wright's work commonly notes that his prose writings center on the figure of the outsider; the novelist focuses on protagonists who either cannot or will not conform to the expectations that figures of authority, whether black or white, impose on them. What concerns me about Wright is not so much that his protagonists are all rebel-victims or outsiders. Rather, I am interested in the strategies his characters use to come to terms with their isolation and their sense of the discontinuity of their lives. My analysis of *Native Son* demonstrates that for Bigger Thomas, the protagonist, as for the autobiographical Richard, learning to tell his own story gives him a measure of control over his life and releases him from his feelings of isolation. Bigger is an uneducated criminal, a far cry from young Richard Wright—the brilliant, sensitive, rather self-righteous budding artist. But both young men are able to heal the discontinuities of their lives by learning to use language to describe themselves.

From the beginning of the novel Bigger's alienation from his oppressive environment is evident. His family and friends—poor, frustrated, brutalized—are tantalized by the promise of the American Dream, a narrative of limitless possibilities that will never be theirs. To mitigate their frustration, Bigger's family and friends all participate in some kind of communal activity. His mother finds consolation in religion, his friends and his girlfriend, Bessie, in drinking. Neither of these particular techniques of evasion satisfies Bigger, although he too seeks a way of alleviating his sense of marginality. As the narrator remarks, "He knew that the moment he allowed himself to feel to its fullness how they lived, the shame and misery of their lives, he would be swept out of himself with fear and despair."[12]

On occasion Bigger avoids his "fear and despair" by blocking out another person's presence. When his family reminds him of their suffering, for example, "he shut their voices out of his mind" (p. 13). When tempted to consider ways of escaping his situation, he "stopped thinking" (p. 16) in order to avoid disappointment. And when at first the Daltons, his white employers, make him feel uncomfortable, Bigger wishes earnestly to "blot" out both himself and "the other[s]" (pp. 49–50; 70).

As his confrontation with his friend Gus shows, Bigger also tries to avoid his own suffering by displacing his self-hatred onto other people. Gus and Bigger argue violently over whether to rob a white-owned store. Bigger fears the consequences both of perpetrating a crime against a white person and of admitting that timidity to his friends. Unable to express his own trepidation, he assaults Gus when he appears reluctant. Bigger recognizes his own fear in Gus's hesitation, and attacks Gus in an effort to destroy it.

Bigger participates in various activities with his friends that insulate him from his fears and insecurities. They rob other black people because they know that to do so will not bring punishment. Moreover, they imagine themselves the protagonists of alternate plots that coincide with the American myth in a way that their own lives do not. When they "play white," for instance, they pretend to be millionaires or public officials, and momentarily forget their own powerlessness. Likewise, they live vicariously through the movies they see. Yet despite this ostensible camaraderie and the lure of fantasy, Bigger is alienated from his friends, for he fears acknowledging his feelings either to himself or to other people. In the words of the narrator: "As long as he could remember [Bigger] had never been responsible to anyone. *The moment a situation became so that it exacted something of him, he rebelled.* That was the way he lived; he passed his days trying to defeat or gratify powerful impulses in a world he feared" (p. 44; emphasis mine).

In order to emphasize Bigger's passivity and fear of articulation in the early sections of the novel, Wright relies on an omniscient narrative presence to tell his reader what Bigger thinks. Since Bigger does not allow himself to think, to act, or to speak directly and openly, the narrator tells us the things Bigger cannot admit to himself, such as his reason for attacking Gus.

Bigger's fear of articulation is also shown in his response to the way strangers talk to him. Bigger is terrified by the Daltons when he arrives at their home. On the surface he seems to be intimidated by their wealth and power. But in fact his disorientation results from his inability to understand their language. When Mrs. Dalton suggests how the family should treat him, she uses a vocabulary that Bigger finds unintelligible and that ironically undercuts the very point she is trying to make: " 'I think it's important emotionally that he feels free to trust his environment,' the woman said. 'Using the analysis contained in the case record the relief sent us, I think we should evoke an immediate feeling of confidence' " (p. 48). Unaccustomed to this kind of speech, Bigger finds her vocabulary threatening: "It made him uneasy, tense, as though there were influences and presences about him which he could feel but not see" (p. 48).

In several ways Bigger's killing of Mary Dalton transforms his personality. The murder, which Bigger has not planned, is ostensibly inadvertent; nevertheless, on a more profound level it is fully intended. Bigger has wanted to "blot" Mary out whenever she has made him feel self-conscious and disoriented. Her murder is therefore important to Bigger because it enables him to complete an action he has willed:

> *He* had done this. *He* had brought all this about. In all of his life this murder was the most meaningful thing that had ever happened to him. He was living, truly and deeply, no matter what others might think, looking at him with their blind eyes. Never had he had the chance to live out the consequences of his actions; never had his will been so free as in this night and day of fear and murder and flight.
>
> (pp. 224–225)

The murder is also profoundly significant because it forces Bigger to confront the fear of the unknown, which has plagued him throughout his life. He and his friends never rob Blum, the white storekeeper, because for them, to commit a crime against a white person is to enter a realm of terror, an area variously referred to by the narrator as "territory where the full wrath of an alien white world would be turned loose upon them" (p. 18), a "shadowy region, a No Man's Land, the ground that separated the white world from the black" (p. 67). It is this unexplored danger zone that Bigger fears and that he persists in avoiding until he kills Mary Dalton. Once he has committed this action, he advances into this gray area, this "No Man's Land"; he realizes that at least initially this trespass has not destroyed him. Indeed, the knowledge that he continues to exist even after he has looked at the heart of darkness empowers him to achieve levels of action and articulation that he had formerly been unable to attain. Having been forced to look directly at that which had frightened him the most, Bigger now begins to liberate himself from the fear that haunts him. Although the murder makes him first a fugitive from and then a prisoner of justice, it initiates the process by which he ultimately comes to understand the meaning of his life.

Because the murder makes Bigger less fearful of the truth, it enables him to understand his environment more clearly. He becomes more analytical, and instead of blotting out his perceptions, he begins to make fine discriminations. Over breakfast on the morning after the murder, for example, he looks at his family as if with new eyes. He sees in his brother's blindness "a certain stillness, an isolation, meaninglessness" (p. 103). He perceives the nuances of his mother's demeanor: "Whenever she wanted to look at anything, even though it was near her, she turned her entire head and body to see it and did not shift her eyes. There was in her heart, it seemed, a heavy and delicately balanced burden whose weight she did not want to assume by disturbing it one whit" (p. 103). And he sees his sister's fear as if for the first time: she "seemed to be shrinking from life in every gesture she made. The very manner in which she sat showed a fear so deep as to be an organic part of her; she carried the food to her mouth in tiny bits, as if dreading its choking her, or fearing that it would give out too quickly" (p. 104).

Moreover, Bigger begins to look at his own life more contemplatively. He interprets what and how his life means by trying to assign value to his past actions. He concludes that the murder was a creative gesture because it has enabled him to refashion his life: "This crime was an anchor weighing him safely in time" (p. 101). In addition, he consciously decides to accept responsibility for an action that might be considered accidental:

Though he had killed by accident, not once did he feel the need to tell himself that it had been an accident. He was black and he had been alone in a room where a white girl had been killed; therefore he had killed her . . . It was no

longer a matter of dumb wonder as to what would happen
to him and his black skin; he knew now. The hidden
meaning of his life—a meaning which others did not see
and which he had always tried to hide—had spilled out.

(p. 101)

Bigger's immediate response to the murder demonstrates
the extent to which it has liberated him and sharpened his
vision. Before the murder Bigger's imagination was in-
hibited by his fears; he generally preferred not to think. Immediately afterward, however, instead of blocking out the
fact of the murder, he confronts and verbalizes it. He has a
momentary impulse to run away, but he denies it. Instead of
lapsing into his characteristically evasive behavior, he begins
to plan his defense with a previously unrevealed freedom of
mind. It would have been simple for Bigger to follow his
first instincts and choose the more passive way out. Earlier in
the evening he had been directed to take Mary's trunk to the
basement before going home for the night. He could have
proceeded as if nothing had gone wrong. He could have
taken the trunk to the basement, put the car in the garage,
and gone home. Instead, he decides to destroy the body and
implicate Mary's boyfriend, Jan. Rather than choosing the
path of least resistance, Bigger creates an elaborate story in
order to save himself.

By identifying Jan (indirectly) as the kidnapper and burn-
ing Mary's body, Bigger actually seeks to return to and
change the past. In a sense, it is as if Bigger takes the pen
from Wright and rewrites his story into the tale he wants it to
be. Bigger removes himself from the role of the protagonist
and changes the nature of the crime to a kidnapping. He tries
to create a substitute reality—that is, a fiction—to replace the
one that threatens to destroy him. The extent of Bigger's
investment in the story he creates is demonstrated in the way

he embellishes it. He keeps searching for a better story, not merely the tightest excuse he can find: "Suppose he told them that he had come to get the trunk?—That was it! The *trunk!* His fingerprints had a right to be there . . . He could take the trunk to the basement and put the car into the garage and then go home. *No!* There was a better way. He would say that Jan had come to the house and he had left Jan outside in the car. But there was still *a better way!* Make them think that Jan did it" (p. 87).[13] The larger significance of Bigger's fiction making and its similarity to young Richard's impulse to write reveals itself if we consider that he has suffered throughout his life from other people's attempts to impose their fictions—stereotypes—on him. Precisely because whites insist on seeing Bigger as less than human, he cannot enjoy the privileges that should be his. Dalton, who is sufficiently myopic to believe that he can be at once a slumlord and a philanthropist, fails to recognize Bigger (or any black person) as fully human. Instead, to him black people are objects of charity easily placated with ping-pong tables. His wife responds to Bigger as if he were a sociological case study. And although Mary and Jan pride themselves on their radical politics, they never really see Bigger either. They treat him as if he and his people were curiosities. They sing spirituals and use black colloquialisms in order to exhibit their familiarity with what are to them exotic artifacts. They insist on eating with Bigger at a black-owned restaurant, oblivious to the discomfort that may cause him. That Jan and Mary use Bigger as a means of access to certain experiences, with no awareness of his feelings, shows that they too see Bigger as their own creation, not as what Bigger himself actually is.

Bigger's misrepresentation in court and in the press epitomizes his lifelong struggle against other people's fictions. Buckley, the State's Attorney, considers him to be violent and subhuman and prosecutes him according to collectively held stereotypes of black male behavior. To him the specific details of Bigger's case are uninteresting, irrelevant. Bigger is guilty of one count of second-degree murder (Mary's) and one count of first-degree murder (Bessie's). The States Attorney, however, considers Bessie's murder significant only insofar as it provides evidence that he can use to reconstruct Mary's death. He successfully prosecutes Bigger for raping Mary on the assumption that black men are driven to possess white women sexually. Moreover, he assumes that Bigger killed Mary to hide the fact that he had raped her. The press similarly denies Bigger's individuality, referring to him with such epithets as "jungle beast" and "missing link" (p. 261). Indeed, the journalists insist that Bigger, a black man, could not be smart enough to have committed his crimes without the assistance of white co-conspirators. They argue that communists helped him plot his crime, because "the plan of the murder and kidnapping was too elaborate to be the work of a Negro mind" (p. 229).

Bigger's complex defense signals his ability to articulate a story about himself that challenges the one that others impose on him. But his story has its limitations and does not accomplish all that Bigger intends. At this stage in his life, he, like the young Richard Wright, recognizes that language has power, but he does not yet know how to use it.

In his naiveté Bigger patterns his tale on pulp detective fiction (p. 87). The story, based on poorly written models, depends on too many narrative inconsistencies. Bigger does not, for example, remember that Jan left him and Mary in order to go to a party and will therefore have an alibi. What is perhaps more important, however, is that Bigger's first story (like the ex-colored man's narrative) fails him because he uses it as a technique of evasion. Although his experience has helped him face his situation, he uses his story to help him escape it.

As I have pointed out, during the period when Bigger is most timid and self-protective (before he arrives at the Dalton home), his consciousness is most restrained, and Wright relies on an omniscient narrator to explain his character's thoughts and motivations. As Bigger's imagination and emotions spring to life, ironically after he kills Mary, Wright relies increasingly on free indirect discourse. In other words, as Bigger's capacity to understand and express himself increases, Wright allows him to speak for himself. Even though Bigger is terrified by the thought of seeing Mary's bones, for example, he can at least acknowledge his fear; he has moved beyond the point of denying his trepidation. As a result, Wright presents his consciousness by approximating Bigger's thoughts:

He stood a moment looking through the cracks into the humming fire, blindingly red now. But how long would it keep that way, if he did not shake the ashes down? He remembered the last time he had tried and how hysterical he had felt. He must do better than this . . . For the life of him, he could not bring himself to shake those ashes. But did it really matter? No . . . No one would look into the bin. Why should they? (p. 161)

Similarly, Bigger comprehends the significance of his inability to retrieve his money from Bessie's dress pocket after he has thrown her down the air shaft: "*Good God!* Goddamn, yes, it was in her dress pocket! Now, he was in for it. He had thrown Bessie down the air-shaft and the money was in the pocket of her dress! What could he do about it? Should he go down and get it? Anguish gripped him . . . He did not want to see her again . . . Well, he would have to do without money; that was all" (p. 224).

As long as Bigger is a fugitive from the law, he thinks

quickly and improvises plans to remain free. When his capture is imminent and Bigger realizes that his future will be even more closely confined than his past, his earlier fears descend on him again and he resumes his former passive, evasive behavior. When his pursuers corner him, Bigger gives up his sense of wholeness and returns to his earlier unresponsiveness. Gradually he steps outside of himself, watching his capture as if from behind a curtain and then ignoring it as if he is standing behind a wall (p. 250). As his captors drag him downstairs, he completes this dissociation by forcing himself to lose consciousness.

Bigger tries but fails to pass his final days in this unresponsive condition. At first he refuses to eat, to drink, to smoke, to resist, and "steadfastly [refuses] to speak" (p. 254). He tries to avoid thinking and feeling as well, because he assumes that his one leap of faith has caused his defeat: "Why not kill that wayward yearning within him that had led him to this end? He had reached out and killed and had not solved anything, so why not reach inward and kill that which had duped him?" (p. 255). When he is bombarded with faces and with the reality of his situation, Bigger faints at his inquest. But when he regains consciousness a second time, his recently acquired sense of himself (the narrator calls it "pride," p. 259) returns, and Bigger begins to rebuild that bridge of words that once connected him with other people. He insists on reading a newspaper because he cannot understand his position until he knows what others are saying about him. More important than his reading, however, are the conversations Bigger has with Jan, Buckley, and Max, the attorney from the Labor Defenders who is in charge of Bigger's defense. Each interview or exchange teaches him something about communication and about himself.

In his conversation with Jan, Bigger conquers his fear of self-scrutiny. Indeed, in his subsequent conversations he attempts to use language to make himself understood with the same clarity he achieves with Jan. By admitting that he and Mary had humiliated Bigger inadvertently, and by offering to help him, Jan enables Bigger to overcome his defenses. His words take Bigger outside of himself and allow him to feel his humanity.

This conversation restores and heightens Bigger's faith in the power of language. Because of this exchange, Bigger does not retreat from his family when they visit him. Instead, he searches for the right words both to comfort them and to defy the authorities. His first attempt to speak to them is unsatisfactory: he tries to dismiss cavalierly the extremity of his situation. But his conversation with Jan has impressed upon Bigger the necessity of candor; Bigger retracts these defensive comments, replacing them with words that express his resignation.

His confession to Buckley teaches Bigger an additional lesson about the necessity of articulation. Buckley's interrogation consists essentially of a series of true-or-false questions. He accuses Bigger of numerous crimes and tries to make him confess to them. Because Buckley seems so eager to pin offenses on him that he never committed, Bigger is forced to defend himself and tell his story as it happened. The effect of articulating this story to a hostile listener drains Bigger; he fears that he may have made himself excessively vulnerable by telling his enemy the truth. But as the narrator suggests, the ostensible ordeal of telling his story actually propels Bigger on to a higher level of self-knowledge:

He lay on the cold floor sobbing; but really he was standing up strongly with contrite heart, holding his life in his hands, staring at it with a wondering question. He lay on the cold floor sobbing; but really he was pushing forward with his puny strength against a world too big and too

strong for him. He lay on the cold floor sobbing; but really
he was groping forward with fierce zeal into a welter of
circumstances which he felt contained a water of mercy for
the thirst of his heart and brain.   (p. 288)

If Bigger's confession to Buckley is important because it
enables him to tell what really happened, his confession to
Max in a parallel scene is important because it enables him
to tell why it happened. Talking to Max allows Bigger to
understand for the first time the complex feelings he had for
Mary. The search for the appropriate words is a painful and
gradual one for him; remembering Mary triggers "a net of
vague, associative" memories of his sister. And ultimately, he
gives up "trying to explain" his actions logically and reverts
"to his feelings as a guide in answering Max" (p. 324). But as
he traces his thoughts and anxieties, Bigger becomes conscious for the first time of certain feelings, and he expresses to
Max emotions that had been intensely private. For example,
during this conversation he first understands the relationship
between the frustration he has always felt and his violence
toward Mary. Moreover, on this occasion he admits to
someone else that he lost control of himself at the moment he
killed Mary. Most important, he is able to explain the value
of the murder: that it freed him from his lifelong fears. While
Bigger felt helpless and betrayed after confessing to Buckley,
explaining himself to Max gives him an enormous sense of
relief. That "urge to talk" had been so strong within him that
he had felt "he ought to be able to reach out with his bare
hands and carve from naked space the concrete solid reasons
why he had murdered" (p. 323). Telling his story helps him
understand those reasons and grants him a "cold breath of
peace" that he had never known before (p. 333).
    Wright's protagonists tend to fit a particular mold. Fish-
burn notes that the protagonists of Wright's later writings are

all patterned after his autobiographical identity: "The young Richard Wright, like all his later heroes, must wrench his identity from a hostile environment; neither Wright nor his heroes have the comfort of being accepted by their own race. All are aliens among both the whites and the blacks."[14] And in "Self-Portraits by Richard Wright," John M. Reilly comments that in *Black Boy* and "The Man Who Lived Underground," "a common viewpoint is that of the outsider in defensive flight from forces in the environment that threaten the personality."[15]

Certainly Bigger suffers alienation from blacks and whites in the way that the autobiographical persona of *Black Boy* and *American Hunger* does. I would suggest a further parallel, however: like this other protagonist, Bigger comes to understand the power of language as a means of creating an identity for himself in an alien environment. Young Richard achieves the greater success; his talent for writing liberates him from the oppression of both the black and the white communities. But Bigger develops the capacity to use language as a way of confronting directly the truths of his own experience. Although it does not save him from electrocution, the capacity to explain himself to others provides him with an awareness of what his life has meant.

FOUR

Ellison's Invisible Autobiographer

In Ralph Ellison's essays and interviews, the artist is a figure of rebellion. Whether writing generally of the role and responsibilities of the contemporary American novelist or of his own specific achievements, Ellison describes the artist always in opposition to the restraints of received literary convention. In "Brave Words for a Startling Occasion," for instance, the text of his acceptance speech for the 1953 National Book Award, he identifies some of the restrictions that limit modern American fiction. For him neither the "tight, well-made Jamesian novel" nor the "hard-boiled novel" can contain the complexity of American life:

There was also a problem of language, and even dialogue, which, with its hard-boiled stance and its monosyllabic utterance, is one of the shining achievements of twentieth-century American writing. For despite the notion that its rhythms were those of everyday speech, I found that when compared with the rich babel of idiomatic expression around me, a language full of imagery and gesture and rhetorical canniness, it was embarrassingly austere.[1]

In response to these constraints, he suggests that the contemporary novelist assume an adversarial posture; he or she must "challenge the apparent forms of reality—that is, the fixed manners and values of the few, and to struggle with it until it reveals its mad, vari-implicated chaos, its false faces, and on until it surrenders its insight, its truth."[2]

Likewise, in his famous rebuttal to Irving Howe's "Black Boys and Native Sons," entitled "The World and the Jug" (1963–64), Ellison describes his objections to protest fiction as practiced by Richard Wright and endorsed by Howe and other critics and reviewers. Finding the vision of Negro life expressed in the genre to be overly narrow and sociological, he defends his right to create novels that "celebrate human life and therefore are ritualistic and ceremonial at their core. Thus they would preserve as they destroy, affirm as they reject."[3] Locating himself in the tradition of American literary craftsmen and moral writers like Twain, Faulkner, Hemingway, and T. S. Eliot, he denies his intellectual links with and debt to earlier black writers.

The assumptions behind Ellison's formulations have jeopardized his credibility with more ideological writers and scholars. Black Aestheticians such as Addison Gayle, Jr., argue that by emphasizing the universality of his work and vision, Ellison eschews the specific political responsibilities of the black writer.[4] Offering a more subtle indictment, Donald B. Gibson demonstrates that although Ellison denies the political implications of his work, *Invisible Man* is nonetheless "a social document that supports certain values and disparages or discourages others, and as such it must take its place among other forces that seek to determine the character of social reality."[5] Perhaps most generously, Houston A. Baker, Jr., shows that although in his essays Ellison values the tradition of Western, literary art over folklore, his novel actually breaks down the distinction between the two modes of creative discourse and celebrates the black expressive tradition.[6]

The politics of Ellison's rhetoric of rebellion are obviously murky, too complicated to untangle here. His critical writing is replete with images of struggle, subversion, iconoclasm; yet he defends a dissociation of art from politics that is arguably reactionary. I share Baker's sense of the complex relation between the ideology of the essays and the novel. But in at least one way the essays may inform our reading of the fiction: the character of the artist in Ellison's nonfiction corresponds with the portrait of the protagonist of *Invisible Man*.

More than just a failed college student, factory worker, and public speaker, Ellison's invisible man is also an artist. His product: the novel that, like Johnson's, presents itself as a simulated autobiography. My analysis will show that, like the artist figure in the essays, the fictional protagonist uses his literary talent to subvert his subordinate relation to figures of authority, to expand the overly restrictive conceptions of identity that others impose on him. As Ellison himself has often remarked, the novel is in no way the story of his own life.[7] Yet onto his protagonist he projects his own sense of the artist's power and responsibility. His characterization of the writer in his nonfiction can thus provide terms by means of which we may assess the power and development of the invisible man.

One might describe the story of Ellison's protagonist as the quest for an appropriate identity. Throughout his life he encounters figures of authority—Norton, Bledsoe, the Brotherhood—who impose false names or unsuitable identities upon him. His experiences teach him that the act of naming is linked inextricably to issues of power and control. When he attempts to live according to the dictates of others, he loses his autonomy and suffers repeated betrayals. He discovers the true meaning of his life only after he assumes responsibility for naming himself by telling his own story.

Inasmuch as it links the narrative act to the achievement of identity, *Invisible Man* (1952) revoices the structures of the slave narrative, of Johnson's *Autobiography,* and of Wright's *Native Son.* Like his counterparts in the earlier novels discussed here, the invisible man enjoys privileges unavailable to his ancestors in bondage. Yet he, like them, is subject to subtle, pernicious forms of injustice and oppression. The image of invisibility recalls the ex-colored man's anonymity and Bigger Thomas's alienation. The very fact of his blackness renders him nonexistent to his superordinates, both black and white. Moreover, his willingness to capitulate to ideology implicates him in his own oppression. Like his predecessors in the tradition, he must assume responsibility for the narrative of his past and future before he can control and believe in the authenticity of his identity.

ॐ

The narrator's dying grandfather, a half-mad war veteran, and Dr. Bledsoe, his college president, all warn him in his youth that since the world deceives, he must also learn to be deceptive. Speaking in elliptical paradoxes to express an ostensibly self-contradictory message, the grandfather advises his family to follow his example and undermine the system while pretending to uphold it: "I want you to overcome 'em with yeses, undermine 'em with grins, agree 'em to death and destruction, let 'em swoller you till they vomit or bust wide open . . . Learn it to the younguns."[8] Dr. Bledsoe attributes his success to a similar ability to feign humility. Astonished by the young protagonist's ignorance of "the difference between the way things are and the way they're supposed to be" (p. 139), Bledsoe shares the grandfather's belief in duplicity as a necessary precondition for achievement. Likewise, the veteran recognizes the world's deceptions. He too tells the protagonist that he must recognize pretense and learn to be duplicitous: "Learn to look beneath the surface . . . Come out of the fog, young man. And remember you don't have to be a complete fool in order to succeed. Play the game, but don't believe in it—that much you owe yourself . . . Learn how it operates, learn how you operate" (p. 151).

The invisible man trivializes this recurring lesson until he suffers repeatedly the consequences of trusting others too readily. He deludes himself into thinking that he is shrewd enough to play whatever game is required of him without believing in it. As if to belie his supposed worldliness, however, his undertakings backfire and reveal him for the bumpkin he is. Only after his trust is abused repeatedly does he understand just how false a face the world presents.

Feigning sophistication, the invisible man says, for example, that he doesn't believe in the principles he articulates in his valedictory address, "that humility [is] the secret, indeed, the very essence of progress" (p. 17). He thinks that he believes only that the semblance of humility works. The embarrassments he suffers, however, show that he lacks sufficient irony about himself and about the nature of authority to distinguish between what is and what works. Lacking any alternative values he can call his own, he invests more of himself than he realizes in the principles he espouses.

The protagonist displays none of his avowed skepticism at the time of the "battle royal." To him, the invitation to speak before "a gathering of the town's leading white citizens" is unparalleled—"a triumph for [the whole black] community." He expects that the occasion will be somber and dignified, and that once he delivers his oration, the audience will "judge truly [his] ability" and reward him (p. 25). The scenario the protagonist envisages reveals his sense that his speech, his polish, and his talent have rendered him superior to his peers. But the actual episode resembles only in its basic outline the one that he anticipates.

The gathering turns out to be a bacchanal. He finds that several black boys his age have been invited to the affair to fight each other; his oratorical skills notwithstanding, he is expected to fight with the others for the audience's entertainment. During the course of the evening the young men are made to watch a nude white woman dance, to fight each other blindfolded, and to dive for counterfeit gold coins on an electrified rug. Each ordeal is designed to mock them. Yet the invisible man hardly recognizes the disparity between his expectations and the actual situation. He resents fighting in the battle royal not because the match itself is degrading, but because he is repelled by the notion of being lumped together with the other black boys. He fears that the association will "detract from the dignity of [his] speech" (p. 17).

When the white guests ask him to speak at the end of the evening, the protagonist is as determined to impress them as he was when he first arrived at the hotel. Without a second thought he resolves to recite every word and to observe each intonation as he had practiced them. His meticulous delivery and posture are at best out of place, if not entirely ludicrous, directed as they are at a noisy and disrespectful crowd. But the protagonist is so convinced of the "rightness of things" (p. 30) that he does not even risk offending his audience by spitting out his bloody, salty saliva. The mere possibility of a reward justifies any insults and indignities to which he may be subjected.

The invisible man might have learned from the battle royal episode to mistrust appearances. He might have begun to suspect the power elite at large when his audience treated him rudely. But the briefcase and scholarship he receives for delivering his speech eclipse all the unpleasantness and confirm his assumption that if he does what the world expects of him, he will be rewarded with respect and acceptance. This belief in a reliable relation between cause and effect proves that he is neither the artificer nor the skeptic he pretends to be but is instead fully confident that things are what they appear and that material rewards await the virtuous.

In college he becomes further committed to this version of the American Dream. He and his fellow students virtually worship the administration and trustees, symbols of all that the college stands for. Millionaires all, these men embody the material success that supposedly ensues from hard work and clean living:

> Here upon this stage the black rite of Horatio Alger was performed to God's own acting script, with millionaires come down to portray themselves; not merely acting out the myth of their goodness, and wealth and success and power and benevolence and authority in cardboard masks, but themselves, these virtues concretely! Not the wafer and the wine, but the flesh and the blood, vibrant and alive, and vibrant even when stooped, ancient and withered. (p. 109)

Dr. Bledsoe provides an even more consistently visible image of what the students' best efforts may yield. His story typifies the standard rags-to-riches formula: he arrived at the college barefoot, motivated by "a fervor for education," and distinguished himself initially by being "the best slop dispenser in the history of the school" (p. 114).[9] After years of hard work he became not only president of the school but a nationally prominent leader as well. In the following description the protagonist betrays his own mythification of Bledsoe and his inability to distinguish between material reward and moral virtue. The passage, conspicuously lacking in irony, juxtaposes achievements and possessions. Political influence, leadership, and Cadillacs are functionally equivalent; moreover, a light-skinned wife ranks as an acquisition along with these other "possessions": Bledsoe "was the example of everything I hoped to be: Influential with wealthy men all over the country; consulted in matters concerning the race; a leader of his people; the possessor of not one, but *two* Cadillacs, a good salary and a soft, good-looking and creamy-complexioned wife" (p. 99).

The protagonist only glimpses the emotional life beneath Bledsoe's obsequious, restrained demeanor after he returns Norton, a white trustee, to the campus. Having been entrusted with the responsibility of showing Norton the area around the college, the protagonist inadvertently introduces him to Trueblood, a black sharecropper who once committed incest with his daughter. He then takes Norton to a bar, the Golden Day, where the trustee is assaulted by prostitutes and mentally disabled war veterans. The protagonist hopes that Bledsoe will understand his situation; instead, he encounters the president's fury.

During their second meeting Bledsoe asks the protagonist why he did not lie to Norton to avoid showing him Trueblood's shack. The protagonist's response betrays his naiveté; he seems barely to know what the verb *to lie* means. Duplicity is so foreign to him that he cannot formulate a sentence of which he is the subject, *to lie* is the verb, and a white person is the direct object: "Lie, sir? Lie to him, lie to a trustee, sir? Me?" (p. 137).

Upon realizing that Bledsoe intends to break his promise to Norton and punish him, the protagonist completely loses control of himself. He dimly perceives that if Bledsoe can break his promise to a trustee and reprimand him for something that was not his fault, then contradictions and accidents can happen, and expected effects will not always follow from causes. The protagonist does not want to believe that inconsistencies are possible, however. In an almost surreal sequence he makes himself reinterpret the meaning of his escapades with Norton, Trueblood, the veteran, and Bledsoe. He forces himself to recast the events in such a way that he is responsible for Norton's misadventure, and that his punishment makes sense. He would rather misunderstand his own experience than see it as a lesson about the disjunction between the way things are and the way they are supposed to be.

Just after he learns of what he thinks of as his "suspension" from college, the protagonist leaves Bledsoe's office and wanders back to his dormitory in a virtual delirium. As a symptom of his inability to accept Bledsoe's sentence, he vomits outside the administration building, realizing to his horror that the world around him has literally gone out of focus. In order to restore his normal vision, he covers one of his eyes; by partially blinding himself, he is able to make his way back to his room.

This episode corresponds symbolically with the invisible man's response to what becomes his expulsion from college. His visual distortion provides an emblem of his brief recognition that his experiences with Norton and Bledsoe have disconfirmed his expectations. For a moment he realizes that his expectations may be fulfilled predictably in his imagination but that the real world operates according to rules that elude him, if indeed it follows any rules at all. But as he covers one eye to avoid seeing double images, so does he consciously deny the distinction between his expectations and reality. He convinces himself that he was at fault and deserves his suspension; he recasts the earlier sequence of events so that they will explain the outcome logically: "Somehow, I convinced myself, I had violated the code and thus would have to submit to punishment. Dr. Bledsoe is right, I told myself, he's right; the school and what it stands for have to be protected. There was no other way, and no matter how much I suffered I would pay my debt as quickly as possible and return to building my career" (p. 145).

When the protagonist pledges to "pay [his] debt as quickly as possible and return to building [his] career," he assumes that his future success will at least diminish by contrast, if not justify, his present suffering. To put it another way, he expects that the passage of time will convert his humiliation into a mere rite of passage. Such a progressive or linear vision of time is fundamental to both the American Dream and the myth of racial uplift; moreover, it is the cornerstone on which the college was founded. Norton tells the protagonist, for example, that the students are his fate. Their accomplishments in the future will validate and render meaningful his past and present efforts: "Through you and your fellow students I become, let us say, three hundred teachers, seven hundred trained mechanics, eight hundred skilled farmers, and so on. That way I can observe in terms of living personalities to what extent my money, my time and my hopes have been fruitfully invested" (p. 45).

As the protagonist exchanges single- for "double-çonsciousness," however, he acknowledges the limitations of his temporal construct.[10] It encourages an investment in the opportunities and possibilities of the future at the expense of the lessons of the past. During the narrative he becomes increasingly able to consider his past experience and learn its lessons.[11] Writing his autobiography shows clearly that for him, retrospection has acquired value. But only after his second major disillusionment does he come to this realization.

During his early days in New York City, the protagonist remains deeply convinced of the rightness of linear vision, of following "the path placed before [him]" (p. 144). The patterns of his thinking display his eagerness to project into the future, his reluctance to reflect. He imagines circumstances that will justify his disgrace. He avoids thinking about his past, however. In his room in the Men's House, for instance, he puts aside the Bible because it makes him homesick and he has no time for nostalgia: "This was New York. [He] had to get a job and earn money" (p. 159). Similarly, when he inadvertently remembers his anger at being expelled, he "hastily" (p. 160) blocks it out. Instead of acknowledging his resentment, he conjures up a future that will redeem his humiliation, one in which he will be Bledsoe's assistant: "In my mind's eye . . . [Bledsoe] was joined by another figure; a younger figure, myself; become shrewd, suave and dressed not in somber garments (like his old-fashioned ones) but in a dapper suit of rich material, cut fashionably, like those of the men you saw in magazine ads, the junior executive types in *Esquire*" (pp. 160–161).

The protagonist intends to find a job in New York by observing professional protocol conscientiously. Well-groomed, prompt, and articulate, he expects that he will easily find suitable employment. Ironically, despite his attempt to manipulate his appearance, it is he, not the prospective employers, who is taken in by appearances. He trusts his letters of reference because of superficial, inconclusive details: he knows that they are about him, and that they are addressed to "men with impressive names" (p. 148). No doubt the watermark and college letterhead make the letters seem all the more trustworthy. But when Emerson, the son of a trustee, shows him the text of the letters, which are in fact critical of him, the protagonist is forced to see that their content is radically at odds with their impressive exterior.

After this revelation, the protagonist recognizes that the values on which the school was founded, those that Bledsoe ostensibly tried to teach him, are spurious. His efforts to humble himself and find employment have backfired; he realizes that this version of the American Dream will never work for him. Once he renounces the goals that have betrayed him, the protagonist begins to behave in freer and more complex ways. His actions during his last visit to the Men's House, for example, symbolize his new-found spontaneity and his thorough separation from his earlier goals. As he looks around the boarding-house lobby, he feels alienated from the upwardly mobile men with whom he had so recently identified himself. He notes, "I now felt a contempt such as only a disillusioned dreamer feels for those still unaware that they dream" (p. 250). By emptying the spittoon over the head of the Baptist preacher he thinks is Bledsoe, he overturns as well the embodiment of his former dreams.

His disillusionment also makes him less defensive about his past. He now tries to consider and learn from his humiliations instead of running from them. On the way home from Emerson's office, he begins to hum a melody that someone near him is whistling. The tune jars his memory and reminds him of a lyric from his childhood:

O well they picked poor Robin clean
O well they picked poor Robin clean
Well they tied poor Robin to a stump
Lawd, they picked all the feathers round from Robin's rump
Well they picked poor Robin clean. (p. 190)

After reconstructing the song, he is able to use its meaning to understand his own situation: he, like "poor Robin," has been picked clean. Previously he would have denied all knowledge of such trivialities as folk rituals and childhood songs; now he sees in them lessons that apply to his condition.

On the morning of his appointment with Emerson, the

invisible man refuses to eat pork chops and grits for breakfast because he wants to avoid being identified with "country" tastes. After he reads Bledsoe's letter, however, he realizes that refined tastes will not necessarily get him anywhere; he therefore begins to accept and follow his impulses more readily. In a reversal of the breakfast episode, the scene in which he buys yams and eats them in public illustrates his heightened self-acceptance, his willingness to savor both the things he enjoys and the memories they conjure up:

> I stopped as though struck by a shot, deeply inhaling, remembering, my mind surging back, back. At home we'd bake them in the hot coals of the fireplace, had carried them cold to school for lunch; munched them secretly, squeezing the sweet pulp from the soft peel as we hid from the teacher behind the largest book, the *World's Geography*. Yes, and we'd loved them candied, or baked in a cobbler, deep-fat fried in a pocket of dough, or roasted with pork and glazed with the well-browned fat; had chewed them raw—yams and years ago. More yams than years ago, though the time seemed endlessly expanded, stretched thin as the spiraling smoke beyond all recall.   (pp. 256–257)

The narrator refers to his immediate postcollege phase as a "period of quietness" (p. 252). He would have done better to call it a "period of inactivity," for although he is unemployed, this is a time of turbulent emotional upheaval for him. When he could rely on a collectively shared set of values or ethics (like the American Dream or the myth of racial uplift), his life was comparatively ordered, and he could feel that he was subscribing to a system of belief that bestowed on him a meaningful identity. The intellectual maneuver he performs to make sense of Bledsoe's punishment shows the lengths to which he will go to fit his experiences into a logically explicable context. He appears resilient, if not placid, because he can contain or freeze his emotional responses, like "ice which [his] life had conditioned his brain to produce" (p. 253). His disillusionment resulting from his conversation with Emerson operates like a "hot red light"; it causes the "ice" to begin to melt, and makes it impossible for him to continue to ignore his feelings. The pain of living at such an intense level of self-awareness makes the protagonist especially susceptible to the influence of the Brotherhood, the Communist party–like organization that he joins, which is committed to the ideals of universal brotherhood and historical change but which minimizes the significance of individual desires and racial specificity. Despite his resolutions, the Brotherhood tempts him irresistibly by offering him a system of beliefs that differs strikingly from the one that deceived him, and promises to restore meaning and thus quiet to his life. Superficial differences notwithstanding, the Brotherhood's ideals prove, of course, to be as unreliable as the American Dream.

The invisible man begins to work for the Brotherhood with the same single-minded faith that he brought to college and to New York. Predictably, his experience with the Brotherhood recapitulates his disaffection from the principles the college embodies. In the Brotherhood, as in college, the invisible man undergoes the ordeal of an undeserved punishment; in both cases he submits and accommodates himself to the sentence. But when the Brotherhood, like his college, betrays his faith a second time, he experiences a revelation and subsequently becomes disillusioned with its ideology.

In order to place his faith unconditionally in the Brotherhood's tenets, the protagonist thinks that he will have to forget the sociology and economics he learned in college (p. 297). In fact he has to forget much more than that. To adhere to the Brotherhood's principles he also has to deny virtually all of the lessons that his college and postcollege experiences have taught him. The Brotherhood's assumptions and tactics are similar to those the protagonist had already rejected; if he had recognized them he might have saved himself some of his despair. But his need for a system of belief and a place to belong is so profound that it blinds him to these resemblances.

The invisible man becomes disaffected from the values Bledsoe represents at least in part because they sacrifice the individual for the system. Considering him utterly insignificant, the college president resolves to destroy the protagonist's career despite his innocence, in order to save the image of the school. The protagonist finds Bledsoe's logic incomprehensible if not nonexistent; he therefore distances himself from the traditional American values Bledsoe embodies in order to preserve or create his own identity.

The Brotherhood similarly considers the interests of the individual insignificant in relation to those of the organization, although unlike Bledsoe it admits this bias overtly. As Brother Jack tells the invisible man at their first meeting, "You mustn't waste your emotions on individuals, they don't count" (p. 284). Tempted by the promise of material and intellectual comfort, the protagonist affiliates himself with the group even though for him individuals (himself in particular) do count. Indeed, his subsequent problems with the Brotherhood arise from this difference of opinion. While he considers it reasonable to follow his own judgment and to try to articulate the concerns of the black community, the Brotherhood finds his behavior divisive and censures him.

The protagonist had learned earlier that his own past experiences, as well as folk traditions, could teach him about his condition. He should therefore have suspected the Brotherhood when it tried to cut him off from his past by changing his name and offering him a "new beginning" (p. 327). But he allows himself to be seduced into the Brotherhood because it provides him with a system of belief that makes individual and political action significant. He cannot resist the hope of finding some meaning in a life and a world that appear chaotic. As he notes in a description of the early days of his Brotherhood career:

> For one lone stretch of time I lived with the intensity displayed by those chronic numbers players who see clues to their fortune in the most minute and insignificant phenomena: in clouds, on passing trucks and subway cars, in dreams, comic strips, the shape of dog-luck fouled on the pavements. I was dominated by the all-embracing idea of Brotherhood. The organization had given the world a new shape, and me a vital role. We recognized no loose ends, everything could be controlled by our science. (p. 373)

The protagonist's eagerness to escape his past and begin his life anew dooms him to repeat his earlier mistakes. Understandably he would like to forget his suffering, humiliation, and cynicism. As he remarks before his first Brotherhood speech, "If I were successful . . . I'd be on the road to something big. No more flying apart at the seams, no more remembering forgotten pains" (p. 327). But when he forgets his pains, he also loses his ironic perspective on figures of authority and makes himself vulnerable once again to their mistreatment.

Indeed, he consciously stops himself from looking at the organization with any skepticism, as if being in the group but not of it would be only disloyal and not self-protective as well:

> I would have to take that part of myself that looked on with remote eyes and keep it always at the distance of the

campus, the hospital machine, the battle royal—all now far behind. Perhaps the part of me that observed listlessly but saw all, missing nothing, was still the malicious arguing part; the dissenting voice, my grandfather part; the cynical, disbelieving part—the traitor self that always threatened internal discord. Whatever it was, I knew that I'd have to keep it pressed down. (p. 327)

As a result he does not (or will not) recognize the Brotherhood's mistreatment of him. He is as innocent of Brother Wrestrum's accusations as he was of Bledsoe's. As he did in the president's office, the protagonist initially explodes when he hears of his punishment. But he accommodates himself yet again to the will of his superior so that he will not be forced to question the institution's ideology. He needs so desperately to trust the Brotherhood that he convinces himself that the reprimand and reassignment are signs of their faith in, not their displeasure with, him:

After all, I told myself, the assignment was also proof of the committee's goodwill. For by selecting me to speak with its authority on a subject which elsewhere in our society I'd have found taboo, weren't they reaffirming their belief both in me and in the principles of Brotherhood, proving that they drew no lines even when it came to women? They had to investigate the charges against me, but the assignment was their unsentimental affirmation that their belief in me was unbroken. (p. 398)

The sequence of events that culminates in Tod Clifton's murder precipitates the invisible man's thorough and lasting reexamination of himself and his relation to authority and ideology. When he sees Clifton selling Sambo dolls on the street corner, the protagonist assumes that he must have been mad to leave the Brotherhood (representing ostensible order and meaning) for such a degrading and meaningless endeavor: "Why should a man deliberately plunge out of history and peddle an obscenity," he asks himself. "Why should he choose to disarm himself, give up his voice and leave the only organization offering him a chance to 'define' himself?" (p. 428). As he considers the nature of Clifton's wares and the fact of his death, however, the protagonist begins to question this formulation. He considers what he and the Brotherhood mean by "history" and acknowledges that the record in which they jointly believe is selectively and arbitrarily preserved; the Brotherhood's ideology is, therefore, no more sacrosanct than any other. Moreover, he begins to question the significance of blacks as a race within the Brotherhood's historical construct, given that its spokesmen persistently deny the importance of race as a category of distinction. The sight of other young blacks causes him to realize that his devotion to the Brotherhood has alienated him from the needs of his people. He remarks that Clifton "knew them better" (p. 432) than he; presumably his inability to reconcile the people's needs with the Brotherhood's forced Clifton to abandon the organization. Once the protagonist perceives that the Brotherhood has ignored the interests of the race, it becomes clear (although it is not explicitly stated in the text) that Clifton's Sambo dolls are not randomly selected products to be hawked on the streets. The black caricatures dangled on a string are, instead, metaphors for the black members of the Brotherhood who are manipulated, unknowingly, by the white leadership.

The invisible man plans a public funeral for Clifton in the hope of organizing the black community in response to this particularly sensitive incident, the shooting of an unarmed black man by a policeman. The construction he places on Clifton's murder differs markedly from the Brotherhood's because it places such a premium on the fact of race. For the protagonist it is more politically significant that Clifton was black than it is that he was a defector from the organization. Moreover, he is more concerned with organizing the black community than he is with preserving the integrity of the Brotherhood's public image. The Brotherhood spokesmen, in contrast, see Clifton's death primarily as the murder of a traitor, an event that concerns them only minimally. They therefore rebuke the protagonist for organizing a hero's funeral. To their minds, faithfulness to the cause is more important than race.

The Brotherhood's response to Clifton's death and funeral confirms the invisible man's worst fears about the organization.[12] Within the Brotherhood he is as invisible as he was in his hometown and at his college. He is significant to Brother Jack and the other leaders only to the extent that he effectively and obediently articulates the party line. Outside of his narrowly defined role within the organization, he does not exist for them. He had mistakenly thought that by upholding the Brotherhood's ideology, he would find purpose and meaning for his life. Clifton's death and his reprimand show him, however, that his life will derive meaning from the platform only if he renounces the prior claims of his own judgment, his own priorities, and, incidentally, his own race. To put it another way, he will have an identity in the Brotherhood only if he concedes the possibility of creating the meaning of his life for himself.

The protagonist's mistrust of the Brotherhood precipitates a period of reflection for him. This betrayal reminds him of the other people who have betrayed him in similar ways. Like Norton and Bledsoe, Jack and the others treat him as if he does not exist. Each man needs to think of him in a certain way, and thus sees only the image he projects:

Here I had thought [the Brotherhood] accepted me because they felt that color made no difference, when in reality it made no difference because they didn't see either color or men . . . [All the people who betrayed him] were very much the same, each attempting to force his picture of reality upon me and neither giving a hoot in hell for how things looked to me. I was simply a material, a natural resource to be used. (p. 497)

His betrayal also prompts him to remember his grandfather's admonition; as he did at the beginning of the narrative, so he resolves at the end to undercut the game (this time the Brotherhood's) even as he pretends to play it.

He reverts to his earlier attempt at duplicity at least in part because he discovers accidentally that he can manipulate his appearance to his advantage. Afraid of being recognized and beaten by the followers of Ras the Exhorter, the Garveylike black nationalist, the protagonist dons sunglasses and a hat only to find that all of Harlem now thinks that he is Rinehart, the quintessential hustler. He realizes that by altering his appearance minimally, he is able to circumvent the problems of being himself and revel in the freedom of being someone else.

The invisible man's experience of betrayal has caused him to believe that no institution, no ideology, is wholly reliable. Given his sense of the world's unreliability, the identity of Rinehart seems to suit him, for Rinehart is a consummate manipulator of surfaces: pimp, numbers runner, lover, and preacher, he is all things to all people. The protagonist finds the idea of Rinehart appealing on two grounds. First, Rinehart provides him with an identity into which he can escape with ease. Second and more important, by being able to change identities at will, he can turn the ephemeral nature of the world to his advantage. He remarks on the place of a Rinehart in a chaotic society: "What is real anyway? . . . The world in which we lived was without boundaries. A vast seething, hot world of fluidity, and Rine the rascal was at home. Perhaps *only* Rine the rascal was at home in it. It was unbelievable, but perhaps only the unbelievable could be believed. Perhaps the truth was always a lie" (p. 487).

The protagonist thinks that by following the example of his grandfather (of which Rinehart is an extreme instance) and feigning compliance, he will protect himself from further deception and acquire some authority over his own life. This experiment works for a time. He reinstates himself in the Brotherhood's good graces by telling its leaders only those things about Harlem that the group wishes to hear—that increased numbers of black people are joining the ranks, for example—and generally affecting a submissive demeanor. At the scene of the Harlem riot, however, he discovers that his false acquiescence has backfired. Because the leaders have withheld the full complexity of their platform, he has been implicated in a conspiracy of which he knew nothing. He had intended to organize the black community; instead, he has been involved unknowingly in the Brotherhood's effort to destroy it: "It was not suicide, but murder. The committee had planned it. And I had helped, had been a tool. A tool just at the very moment I had thought myself free. By pretending to agree I had indeed agreed, had made myself responsible for that huddled form lighted by flame and gunfire in the street, and all the others whom now the night was making ripe for death" (p. 541).

Here the invisible man realizes the implausibility of feigning compliance with an ideology. Because he is necessarily subordinate to figures of authority, he will never know the full nature of their program. Commitment to an ideology requires a leap of faith, a leap he has always been only too willing to make. Yet each time he commits himself, what he leaps over threatens to destroy him.

In other words, what he learns ultimately is that he will never have control over his own life if he tries to play the game but not believe in it. As he notes, he "had been used as a tool. [His] grandfather had been wrong about yessing them to death and destruction or else things had changed too much since his day" (p. 552). His grandfather might have been able to feign compliance while undercutting the system, but the protagonist has repeatedly seen that for him, to comply in part is to comply altogether. He therefore resolves to sever his connections to society, to all the organizations on which he had relied for self-definition, and to accept responsibility for creating his own identity. After his final conference with Brother Hambro he recognizes that if his life is to have any meaning, it must be the sum of all he had undergone. When he retreats underground to write his own story, he commits himself to sifting through those experiences and attributing his own meaning to them.

෴

By choosing to go underground and compose the story of his life, the invisible man shows that he has exchanged one group of mentors—his grandfather, Bledsoe, and the veteran—for another, Trueblood and Brother Tarp.[13] Both groups, whether explicitly or implicitly, warn him against being too trusting. But while the first emphasizes the importance of learning to deceive as he also is deceived, the latter provides models for creating a sense of identity independent of what an organization or a collective set of assumptions requires. Throughout his life the invisible man learns that he can never be deceptive enough. No matter how devious he thinks he is, those who control him always manage to trick and betray him. His efforts at creating an identity simultaneously within and outside an institution therefore seem doomed to failure. When he decides to write his own story, he relinquishes the meaning generated by other ideologies in favor of one that is primarily self-generated. By designating a beginning and an end to his story, he converts events that threaten to be chaotic into ones that reveal form and significance. He creates for himself a persona that develops, indeed exists, in contradistinction to the images that others have projected onto him. Moreover, he inverts his relation to the figures of authority who have dominated him, for as author-narrator he is able to control the identities of such people as Norton, Bledsoe, and Brother Jack. By presenting them in uncomplimentary ways, he avenges the humiliations they have inflicted on him. The double-consciousness of simultaneously playing and undermining the game has proved impracticable. But the solution to the problems of identity and authority can be found in the double-consciousness of reliving his story as both narrator and protagonist.

Brother Tarp and Trueblood both appear to realize that their identity is determined by the sum of complex experiences they have undergone. Each man has a story that defines him in contrast to the identity that others have tried to impose or project. Tarp conceives of himself as the protagonist of the story of his prison experience. Because he "said no to a man who wanted to take something" from him (p. 378), he spent nineteen years in jail and lost his family and his property. He remained in prison until he was able to break free, at which time he determined he could create a new life for himself. The story he tells the invisible man, his inescapable memories, his limp, and the link from his leg iron are all ways in which Tarp keeps his past with him in the present. These things remind him that he is still looking for freedom, and they remind him of those values he holds most dear, those that give his life meaning.

Jim Trueblood also tells a story about a critical experience that reveals his sense of identity. Although the protagonist meets him at a point in the narrative when he can in no way appreciate what the farmer represents, his decision to write his story harks back to Trueblood's tale.[14] Like the protagonist, Trueblood is invisible: no one sees him as he is. Because he has committed incest with his own daughter, blacks consider him a disgrace and whites think of him as a sort of dirty joke. Although others ostracize and ridicule him, Trueblood asserts his own sense of identity by telling and retelling a tale of his own creation. He acknowledges the complexity and ambiguity of his situation: being both guilty and not guilty of incest. As Selma Fraiberg notes, however, instead of allowing myth (or convention) to determine the meaning of his action, Trueblood refuses "to hide behind the cowardly deceptions that cloak sin; he faces the truth within himself."[15] He understands, as the protagonist comes to learn, that he can control the meaning of his life if he converts his experiences into a narrative, thus determining what construction should be placed on them. His well-crafted tale prefigures the protagonist's autobiography, a text that endows with meaning events that seemed random as they were lived, by imposing artistic form on them.[16]

Before beginning his story, Trueblood assumes the stance of the narrator par excellence: "He cleared his throat, his eyes gleaming and his voice taking on a deep incantatory quality, as though he had told the story many, many times" (p. 53). He sets the stage for a complex and subtle story. In order to create the atmosphere of the evening he had intercourse with Matty Lou, he evokes visual, olfactory, and aural images. On that tranquil, critical night, past and present merged for him; he lay in bed with his wife and daughter remembering another peaceful time in his life when he lived with an earlier lover in a house on the Mississippi. He recalls hearing the river boats approach and conjures up the scene with fluid, sophisticated imagery. Human and animal worlds, all the senses, dream and waking life merge. He analogizes the sound of the distant river boats to the "boss bird'" calling the covey together during quail season:

> I'd be layin' there and it would be quiet and I could hear it comin' from way, way off. Like when you quail huntin' and it's getting dark and you can hear the boss bird whistlin' tryin' to get the covey together again, and he's coming toward you slow and whistlin' soft, cause he knows you somewhere around with your gun. Still he got to round them up, so he keeps on comin'. Them boss quails is like a good man, what he got to do he do. (p. 55)

He captures the sound of the boat nearing the house in terms of a visual image that becomes, in turn, aural, gustatory, and then visual again:

> It sounded like somebody hittin' at you slow with a big shiny pick. You see the pick-point comin' straight at you, comin' slow too, and you can't dodge; only when it goes to hit you it ain't no pick a'tall but somebody far away breakin' little bottles of all kindsa colored glass . . . Then you hear it close up, like when you up in the second-story window and look down on a wagonful of watermelons, and you see one of them young and juicy melons split open a-layin' all spread out and cool and sweet on top of all the striped green ones like it's waitin' just for you, so you can see how red and ripe and juicy it is and all the shiny black seeds it's got and all. And you could hear the sidewheels splashin' like they don't want to wake nobody up; and us, me and the gal, would lay there feelin' like we was rich

folks and them boys on the boats would be playin' sweet as
good peach brandy wine.   (p. 55)

His use of synesthesia reveals the heightened sensuality of his
reminiscences. Furthermore, the artistry of his story displays
the extent to which he has shaped the experience linguis-
tically. By following the associative patterns of his thoughts,
he seems to relive the situation as he first experienced it. His
tale is anything but spontaneous, however, for his use of
imagery indicates that he is self-consciously creating the impression (whether true or not) that the atmosphere of the
evening was largely responsible for the act of incest.

Given the sensuality of his ruminations while he lies in bed
awake, it seems logical that he would have an erotic dream
once he falls asleep. As his dream opens he has just violated
custom and entered a white man's house through the front
door. Unintentionally he proceeds to a large white bedroom
and discovers there a white woman dressed in a negligee.
Although he tries to escape, she holds him back. The tension
of the situation is heightened by the grandfather clock, which
strikes faster and faster. When he throws the woman on the
bed "to break her holt," the two of them begin to sink into
her bed: "It's sinkin' down so far I think it's going to smother
both of us. Then swoosh! all of a sudden a flock of little white
geese flies out of the bed like they say you see when you go to
dig for buried money. Lawd! they hadn't no more'n disappeared than I heard a door open and Mr. Broadnax's voice
said, 'They just nigguhs leave 'em do it' " (p. 58). In the next
phase of the dream he runs toward the clock and describes his
entry into it in terms suggestive of the sexual act and climax.

In the first phase of the dream Trueblood transgresses a
series of social taboos: he enters the white man's home by the
front door and has sexual contact with a white woman. Then

the dream landscape changes from the representational to the phantasmagoric. When he awakens, he realizes that his actual situation parallels his dream. In life he has just violated a sexual taboo, albeit that of incest rather than miscegenation. The presence of his wife in the same bed compounds his horror, as the ticking of the clock exacerbates the tension in the dream. Furthermore, he acknowledges in life as well as in the dream the sexual pleasure he derives from the forbidden act.

As Trueblood narrates the sequence of events that ensued, he heightens the reader's sympathy for him by demonstrating both his willingness to accept responsibility for his sin and his attempt to endure his wife's rage. He describes Kate's fury and his readiness to submit to physical punishment at her hand. He even agrees to leave his family for a while. Eventually, however, he insists on returning to them and facing the consequences of his actions. Moreover, he refuses to allow either his wife or his daughter to abort his child, and chases away everyone who tries to stand between him and his family.

During the time Trueblood is away from his family, he tries and fails to explain himself to his minister. Religion cannot accommodate or justify his sin, and thus cannot help him make sense of his behavior. He tries to determine on his own the extent of his guilt, turning the incident over in his mind. Eventually he sings the blues; like his narrative itself, the music he creates allows him, finally, to come to terms with what he has done.

The subtly complex narrative Trueblood constructs replaces the reductive, derogatory version that the townspeople tell. According to his story, because of the ambiance of the evening and the dreams it triggered, he was not fully awake when the sexual encounter with his daughter began. He has sufficient self-respect, however, to assume responsibility for his actions, whether intentional or not. Thus he transforms himself from villain or buffoon to hero by proving simultaneously his innocence and his willingness to accept blame.

Like Trueblood, the invisible man chooses and designs his identity with great care. He rejects the assumption that his past experiences are meaningless and merely sequential in favor of the belief that, taken together, they make up who he is. In his youth he thought that the past was best put at a distance, that identity could be changed at will, and that it could be defined by one's affiliations. By the time he writes the narrative, however, he realizes that all other-imposed identities are false. One's true identity is the sum of one's experiences; therefore, to deny the past is to deny oneself:

> It was as though I'd learned suddenly to look around corners; images of past humiliations flickered through my head and I saw that they were more than separate experiences. They were me; they defined me. I was my experiences and my experiences were me, and no blind men, no matter how powerful they became, even if they conquered the world, could take that, or change one single itch, taunt, laugh, cry, scar, ache, rage or pain of it. (pp. 496–497)

Telling his story allows him to arrange and recount his experiences in such a way as to display the meaning of his life. The beginning and end he chooses, the recurrent patterns he discloses refute the opinion that his life lacks significance and is therefore expendable. He shows through his narrative that there is coherence to his life and method to his humiliations. As he learns the value of increased self-reliance, he develops from naiveté and powerlessness to wisdom and authority.

The invisible man might have selected any incident from his life to open the narrative action of his autobiography. If he had wanted immediately to call his reader's attention to his talents, for example, he might have begun by describing at length the first occasion at which he delivered his valedictory address, his high school graduation. Because he intended the first chapter to create quite a different effect, however, he selected for the first memorable event of the novel one that highlights his naive and overly trusting nature. By essentially beginning the narrative by juxtaposing the battle royal with the valedictory address, he calls the reader's attention to his own myopia and his overdependence on others' values. This beginning guarantees the reader's awareness that these shortcomings will cause his subsequent humiliations.

The narrator focuses on his own limitations at least in part to justify his susceptibility to betrayal. By revealing certain motifs that attend his humiliations, he further shows that some order infuses his experiences even though he was unable to see this when he lived them. For example, as I noted earlier, his betrayal by the Brotherhood recapitulates his betrayal by Bledsoe. The invisible man might have avoided being deceived a second time if he had recognized the techniques of deception and his own credulity from his earlier betrayal. Had he wanted to call the reader's attention to the arbitrariness of his humiliations, he could have presented the story in such a way as to emphasize the differences between the two betrayals. He would then have appeared to be the powerless victim of random, inexplicable circumstances. He highlights both the predictability of organizations and his own culpability, however, by underscoring the similarities between the college and the Brotherhood.

Recounting his story also allows the protagonist to redress the abuses he suffered and to overturn the authority of those who misled him both in college and in the Brotherhood.[17] Although he was unable to confront them in life, as author of the narrative he can deflate the images of those who ridiculed or deceived him by characterizing them as buffoons and villains. He presents Norton and the minister Homer Barbee, for example, with no small degree of irony, in order to undercut the beliefs they profess.

As a student, the invisible man reveres Norton and all that he represents. Rich, shrewd, elegantly attired and exceedingly well mannered, the college trustee embodies everything to which the protagonist aspires. Flattered at having been asked to drive for him, the young man is eager to please, fearful of offending. Characteristically, he expects that if he drives and converses well, he will receive some reward: "Perhaps he'd give me a large tip, or a suit, or a scholarship next year" (p. 38). Indeed, even after the protagonist is "suspended," he thinks that Norton will be able to help him if only he can find him. By the time he writes the narrative, of course, he has ceased to believe either that wealthy white benefactors are necessarily virtuous or that institutions like the school can uplift the race.

As if to retaliate against Norton for his having misled him, the invisible man subtly but unmistakably impugns the motives behind his philanthropy. Norton thinks that he is impelled to support the school by his wish to commemorate his late daughter. The words the narrator attributes to Norton, however, betray his incestuous attraction to her, and imply strongly that his generosity may well be an act of atonement for a sin he fails to acknowledge. When Norton speaks of his daughter, his tone is more that of a bereaved lover than of a father. In addition, he says that he was never able to believe that she was his own, and he expresses an undefined sense of guilt about her. Taken together, these features of his description disclose his problematic relation to her:

"[My daughter] was a being more rare, more beautiful, purer, more perfect and more delicate than the wildest

dream of a poet. I could never believe her to be my own
flesh and blood. Her beauty was a well-spring of purest
water-of-life and to look upon her was to drink and drink
and drink again . . . She was rare, a perfect creation, a
work of purest art . . . I found it difficult to believe her my
own . . .
   "She was too pure for life," he said sadly, "too pure and
too good and too beautiful . . . I have never forgiven
myself."   (p. 42)

Norton's response to Trueblood further indicates that his
daughter may well have had some sexual appeal for him. He
overreacts wildly when he learns that the man has committed
incest with his own daughter and has gone unpunished:
" 'You did and are unharmed!' he shouted, his blue eyes
blazing into the black face with something like envy and
indignation" (p. 51). Trueblood's powerful narrative devas-
tates Norton because it forces him to confront his own
deeply concealed desires. By juxtaposing Norton's and
Trueblood's responses to incest, the narrator reveals the extent of both the farmer's self-awareness and the trustee's lack
of it. When he and Norton meet Trueblood, the protagonist
is so overwhelmed by the white man's image and so worried
about his own that he completely misreads the situation. He
not only overestimates Norton, but he also treats Trueblood
dismissively. In the narrative he corrects this error in judgment. He deposes Norton as a mentor, and by telling his
own tale follows Trueblood's example instead.
   The protagonist is likewise overly impressed by the Reverend Homer Barbee, who preaches a sermon on the evening
of the Trueblood episode. Having jeopardized his college
career, the protagonist is moved to guilty tears by Barbee's
address, for it celebrates all that the school represents. The
minister reminds the students of the legacy of the Founder:

like the school itself, Bledsoe sprang up from nothing and dedicated himself to the progress of the race. Moreover, Barbee praises Bledsoe's benevolence and leadership:

> Your leader has kept his promise a thousandfold. I commend him in his own right, for he is the co-architect of a great and noble experiment. He is a worthy successor to his great friend and it is no accident that his great and intelligent leadership has made him our leading statesman. His is a form of greatness worthy of your imitation. I say to you, pattern yourselves upon him. Aspire, each of you, to some day follow in his footsteps. Great deeds are yet to be performed. (pp. 130–131)

At the time he hears the speech, the protagonist feels so ashamed of himself that he is unable to stay through the service. The speech convinces him for at least a short while that his error has threatened the entire institution. "I could not look at Dr. Bledsoe now, because old Barbee had me both feel my guilt and accept it. For although I had not intended it, any act that enlarged the continuity of the dream was an act of treason" (p. 132).

But looking back at the episode from the end of the narrative, he realizes that the values Barbee articulated are corrupt. The very way in which he notes the minister's blindness mocks his faith in these principles. Since the narrator knows at the time he recounts the episode that Barbee is blind, he might have acknowledged that fact when he first describes the minister's approach to the lectern. If he had wanted to preserve Barbee's image, he might have introduced his speech with a statement like, "His blindness did not detract from the insightfulness of his sermon." Instead, he conceals the fact of his blindness until Barbee has completed his stirring message. He describes his sudden fall, and then explains in two abrupt sentences: "For a swift instant, between the gesture and the opaque glitter of his glasses, I saw the blinking of sightless eyes. Homer A. Barbee was blind" (p. 131). One might argue that he narrates the episode as he does to recapture the sequence of his perceptions. But his motives are more complex than such a reading would suggest. He intends the fall and the disclosure of Barbee's blindness to reflect on the sermon itself. That is, although he did not realize it when he heard the speech, he now knows that Barbee must have been intellectually imperceptive (that is, blind) if he believed what he professed.

Like any autobiographer, the invisible man chooses an ending for his narrative that is logically consistent with the meaning of the story as a whole. As Frank Kermode writes, "The provision of an end [makes] possible a satisfying consonance with the origins and with the middle."[18] He has constructed the tale of his development from ignorance to knowledge of both the meaning of identity and the proper relation to the power elite. It would therefore be to his advantage to end at a point where he is palpably wiser than he was before. The invisible man gives his narrative a cyclical structure, however. He repeatedly thinks that he has figured out how to maneuver his way around figures of authority, only to find that his strategy has failed him. The decision to remove himself from society and write his own story might thus represent only one of an interminable list of strategies. This last seems to differ from the earlier attempts, however, for it appears to require him to depend on himself for the construction of his identity more than his previous ventures did. But since the story ends before he reenters society, the reader never knows to what degree he will conform to institutional expectations once he goes back to the world.

By ending where he does, the invisible man loads the dice in his own favor, one final advantage to telling his own story.

He leaves the reader with his conviction that the double-consciousness of being both narrator of and participant in his own story empowers him in a way that his earlier duplicity did not. Had he ended his story later, this solution might have proven no better than his previous attempts at compliance or deceit. The persona of the narrative present (the voice of the prologue and the epilogue) may seem more sophisticated than the protagonist only because he knows where to stop.

FIVE

ॐ

Toni Morrison's Narratives of Community

In Toni Morrison's first three novels flashbacks abound. Not only do her protagonists' histories find their way into her plots, but the past lives of her minor characters return to haunt as well. Occasionally her characters reminisce in their own voices in midconversation. But more often than not an omniscient voice interrupts the narrative present to tell and interpret a character's personal history. These frequent forays into the past impart to Morrison's novels a kaleidoscopic quality, a temporal density, and an extraordinary breadth of focus.

Flashbacks and shifts in subject are the formal counterparts of Morrison's thematic concerns. This correlation between form and theme is especially evident in *Song of Solomon* (1977), where reminiscences and interpolated stories proliferate within the context of Milkman Dead's journey into history. Morrison suggests that the narrative process leads to self-knowledge because it forces an acceptance of the past. Her characters understand who they are and what their lives mean when they can tell stories about how they came to be. My analysis of her work centers on *Song of Solomon*, the only one of Morrison's novels to examine the actual process by which a character arrives at his or her own story. No discussion of narration in *Song of Solomon* would be complete, however, without a consideration of Morrison's two early novels *The Bluest Eye* (1970) and *Sula* (1973). Her use of interpolated stories in these two works establishes a framework in terms of which we may understand the meaning and status of the stories in *Song of Solomon*.

჻

In *The Bluest Eye* and *Sula* Morrison explores the interplay between self-knowledge and social role. Her characters, like Ellison's invisible man, inhabit a world where inhospitable social assumptions obtain. Yet Morrison does not provide her people with the option of living underground, in isolation, beyond community. Her characters achieve autonomy and a sense of identity only to the extent that they can understand and name themselves in relation to a social unit, be it family, neighborhood, or town. Those whom social relations exclude lack self-knowledge and are destroyed by themselves or by others.[1]

Morrison's black characters are especially vulnerable to the defeat that accompanies isolation; in both of these early novels she examines the complex economic, historical, cultural, and geographic factors that shape their problematic relations within the black community and the world beyond. Pecola Breedlove, on whom Morrison's first novel centers, typifies Morrison's outsiders. Her story illustrates the destructive potential of a culture that recognizes only one standard of physical beauty and equates that standard with virtue. Ostensibly Pecola is driven mad by her inability to have blue eyes. (She loses her mind immediately after the spell cast by Soaphead Church, the neighborhood pedophile, fails to grant her wish.) But her insanity really results from the cumulative weight of her own self-loathing and that of those who project onto her their contempt for themselves. Soaphead Church's failure to give her the blue eyes she wants is thus simply the proverbial back-breaking straw.

The Bluest Eye does not address hard questions directly. The book does not undertake to explain, for example, why black Americans aspire to an unattainable standard of beauty; why they displace their self-hatred onto a communal scapegoat; how Pecola's fate might have been averted. The metaphors of Claudia MacTeer (one of the narrators) that frame and image Pecola's story, and the very structure of the novel itself, suggest that such considerations are unresolvable. "This soil is bad for certain kinds of flowers," Claudia remarks. "Certain seeds it will not nurture, certain fruit it will not bear."[2] Claudia accepts as a given the fact that certain "soils" will reject both marigolds and plain black girls. To her, the reasons for this incompatibility are structural, too complex to decipher. She therefore believes that any attempt to explain Pecola's deterioration will be fruitless, and concludes that *"there is really nothing more to say—except why. But since why is difficult to handle, one must take refuge in how"* (p. 9).

It is not only Claudia but the novel itself that avoids "why" and takes refuge in "how." Claudia, the narrator of the preschool primer with which the novel begins, and the ostensibly omniscient narrator tell stories—tell "how" fast and furiously. In general, these stories demonstrate what it means to find inaccessible the possessions and attributes one's culture values. Because of their thematic similarity, these stories comment on Pecola's story in two ways. First, they indicate that what happens to Pecola is representative, not unique; that self-loathing inevitably leads to some form of destruction. Second, the remarkable number of stories symbolizes the complex sources and effects of this cycle of self-loathing. The form is therefore a figure for the cultural condition the novel addresses.[3]

The two and one-half pages that precede the body of *The Bluest Eye* introduce two of the three narrators. The novel begins with three versions of fourteen lines from the Dick and Jane primer: "Here is the house. It is green and white. It has a red door," and so on. The first version of these lines is punctuated and spaced conventionally; proper names and the initial letter of each sentence are capitalized. The second version contains no punctuation and capitalizes only the first letter of the excerpt; the spacing between the lines has been reduced. In the third and final version all the spaces between the words have been closed up, and the spaces between the lines have been further reduced. These lines from the primer remind us of our earliest reading and call our attention to the vision of American life they establish as normative. Devoid of punctuation and spacing, however, these lines, and by extension the standard they represent, become virtually unintelligible. Morrison thus demystifies the dominant ideology before the novel proper begins.

The voice of the primer is followed by Claudia's brief reminiscence about the period the novel describes. Claudia's remarks frame the novel in that they identify the narrative present as the autumn of 1940 and set up Pecola's story as an example of the kind of tragedy that is hard to explain and yet harder to avert.

The body of the novel is divided into four chapters named for the four seasons. The chapters are, in turn, subdivided. Each begins with an episode, usually involving Pecola, told from the point of view of Claudia the child but shaped by her adult reflections and rhetoric. Claudia's stories then yield place to one or two stories told by an apparently objective, omniscient narrator. This narrator usually recalls information to which Claudia would not have had access, telling stories from Pecola's life that involve other characters and weaving flashbacks from the lives of these other characters into Pecola's story. In addition, in each chapter several garbled lines from the primer separate Claudia's voice from that of the omniscient narrator.

The chapters counterpoise three moments in time: a past before the narrative present (the flashbacks), the eternal present of the primer, and the narrative present of Pecola's story as told by Claudia. The different narratives in each chapter provide variations on a specific theme. More important, this technique demonstrates here and throughout Morrison's fiction the interconnectedness of past and present. The form implies that the meaning of Pecola's story may be understood only in terms of events that predated her birth. There is, in other words, no journeying forward without a journey back. "Winter," the second chapter, illustrates the interplay between the three narrative voices that both elaborates on a particular theme and demonstrates the interconnections between past and present.

At the beginning of "Winter," Claudia recalls the figures of security that she and her family generally associated with that season. Her reminiscences conjure up images of her father and of the home remedies that worked to keep the cold away:

Wolf killer turned hawk fighter, he worked night and day to keep one from the door and the other from under the windowsills. A Vulcan guarding the flames, he gives us instructions about which doors to keep closed or opened for proper distribution of heat, lays kindling by, discusses qualities of coal, and teaches us how to rake, feed, and bank the fire . . .

Winter tightened our heads with a band of cold and melted our eyes. We put pepper in the feet of our stockings, Vaseline on our faces, and stared through dark ice-

box mornings at four stewed prunes, slippery lumps of
oatmeal, and cocoa with a roof of skin.   (p. 52)

Ironically, the events that both Claudia and the omniscient
narrator present in this chapter have not these qualities
of winter but rather the quality of pneumonia weather—
warmth that turns suddenly and relentlessly cold. Claudia
describes a day in which she is disappointed by both a class-
mate she envies and her parents' boarder; the omniscient narrator tells how Pecola is hurt by a woman she admires.

The triumph over a gang of bullies binds the MacTeer
sisters, Pecola, and Maureen Peal together briefly. This
camaraderie is remarkable, since Claudia and Frieda MacTeer
usually scorn Maureen, "the high-yellow dream child with
long brown hair" (p. 52). True to form, the MacTeer sisters
are soon unable to forgive Maureen the things they envy: her
wealth, worldliness, long hair, and fair skin. And when they
begin to taunt her, she makes explicit her contempt for their
dark skin: "I *am* cute! And you ugly! Black and ugly black e
mos. I *am* cute!" (p. 61).[4]

The MacTeers arrive at home that afternoon to be cheered
by their parents' boarder, Mr. Henry, who gives them
money for candy and ice cream. For the second time that day
their pleasure turns to disappointment, however, for they
discover that Mr. Henry has sent them off not out of
generosity but out of self-interest: he wanted to be free to
entertain a pair of prostitutes. Both incidents thus reveal the
potential for coldness and insensitivity that underlies even the
most appealing and inviting facades.

The omniscient narrative voice in this chapter tells of
Pecola's encounter with Junior, one of her black, middle-
class schoolmates, and Geraldine, his mother. The episode
centers on Geraldine, who, like Maureen and Mr. Henry,
represents a false spring. The section begins with the nar-

rator's description of Geraldine's upbringing as a young girl in the South raised to be meticulous, religious, sexless, and unemotional:

> These particular brown girls from Mobile and Aiken are not like some of their sisters. They are not fretful, nervous, or shrill; they do not have lovely black necks that stretch as though against an invisible collar; their eyes do not bite. These sugar-brown Mobile girls move through the streets without a stir. They are as sweet and plain as buttercake. Slim ankles; long, narrow feet. They wash themselves with orange-colored Lifebuoy soap, dust themselves with Cashmere Bouquet talc, soften their skin with Jergens Lotion. They smell like wood, newspapers, and vanilla.
>
> (pp. 67–68)

The narrator tells Geraldine's story as if she were a type, not an individual, in order to emphasize the extent of her assimilation; she is so thoroughly socialized that nothing original remains.

The ensuing flashback from Geraldine's point of view explains the vehemence with which she throws Pecola out of her house. Geraldine's adulthood has been a slow process of eradicating "the funk" (p. 67), the kind of disorder that for her blackness exemplifies. In Pecola's face she confronts the image of all she has tried to escape, and feels as if her private terrain has been invaded:

> She had seen this little girl all of her life. Hanging out of windows over saloons in Mobile, crawling over the porches of shotgun houses on the edge of town, sitting in bus stations holding paper bags and crying to mothers who kept saying "Shet up!" Hair uncombed, dresses falling apart, shoes untied and caked with dirt. They had stared at

her with great uncomprehending eyes. Eyes that questioned nothing and asked everything. Unblinking and unabashed, they stared up at her. The end of the world lay in their eyes, and the beginning, and all the waste in between.

They were everywhere . . . And this one had settled in her house. (p. 75)

Her final words to Pecola recall Maureen's words to Frieda and Claudia: "Get out, . . . You nasty little black bitch. Get out of my house" (p. 75).

The voice of the garbled version of the primer separates Claudia's story from that of the omniscient narrator. Here, as in each of the chapters, these excerpted lines comment ironically on the content of the chapter. In "Winter" we read: "SEETHECATITGOESMEOWMEOWCOMEAND-PLAYCOMEPLAYWITHJANETHEKITTENWILLNOT-PLAYPLAYPLA" (p. 67). The correctly punctuated version of these lines might evoke the cliché of the coy household pet too finicky to play. But the scenario at Geraldine's house to which the lines refer is as jumbled as the lines themselves. For one thing, as the narrator tells us, the cat has replaced both Geraldine's husband and her son in her affections, perhaps because it is cleaner. And the cat is, of course, central to the episode the chapter describes. Junior lures Pecola into his house by promising to let her play with his cat. He tortures and perhaps kills the cat when he finds that it and Pecola are drawn to each other. So if Geraldine's cat will not play, it may well be because it is dead.

This chapter thus shows some of the forms that overinvestment in an alien cultural standard may take. Like Pecola, Maureen and Geraldine yearn to be white. Pecola's aspirations are entirely unattainable, since they take the form of a desire for blue eyes. Maureen and Geraldine aspire to intermediate goals that are for them more easily accessible. But their desires spring from a hatred of what they are that is as profound as Pecola's. By juxtaposing these and other stories to Pecola's, Morrison displays the dimensions of her protagonist's condition.

વ્જ

Sula is centered around a character who believes that she can create for herself an identity that exists beyond the community and social expectations. "An artist with no art form,"[5] Sula uses her life as her medium, "exploring her own thoughts and emotions, giving them full reign, feeling no obligation to please anybody unless their pleasure pleased her" (p. 102). She thus defies social restraints with a vengeance. She disavows gratuitous social flattery, refusing to compliment either the food placed before her or her old friends gone to seed and using her conversation to experiment with her neighbors' responses. As the narrator remarks, "In the midst of pleasant conversation with someone, she might say, 'Why do you chew with your mouth open?' not because the answer interested her but because she wanted to see the person's face change rapidly" (p. 103). Worst of all in her neighbors' judgment, she discards men, black and white, as rapidly as she sleeps with them, even the husband of her best friend, Nel.

There are moments when the text seems to validate Sula's way of life; the narrator suggests, for example, that Sula's independence has bestowed on her a kind of immortality:

Among the weighty evidence piling up was the fact that Sula did not look her age. She was near thirty and, unlike them, had lost no teeth, suffered no bruises, developed no ring of fat at the waist or pocket at the back of her neck. It was rumored that she had had no childhood diseases, was never known to have chicken pox, croup or even a runny nose. She had played rough as a child—where were the scars?

(p. 100)

But finally the novel demonstrates both explicitly and structurally that Sula's attempts to live experimentally are misguided and doomed to failure. It argues that what Sula considers to be an improvisational self is really no self at all. As the narrator remarks, "She had no center, no speck around which to grow" (p. 103). Her unrestrained sexuality thus reflects not an interest in the act for its own sake, but rather a means by which she can experience a sensation profound enough to convince her of her own existence.

The plot and structure of the novel further undercut Sula's notion of independence. On the most obvious level, Sula's inexplicable death demonstrates that within the terms of the novel, her quest for independence is not feasible. Some critics argue that Sula dies because she has lost Ajax, the only man she has tried to possess.[6] To make that case is, I think, to read the last chapter of Sula's story only in the context of her relationship to Ajax, not in the context of her entire life—to overread the juxtaposition, as it were. I would suggest that Sula's story has been a gradual winding down, a series of random, pointless efforts to create a self. These gestures lead inevitably to her death either because Morrison wants to prove the futility of such a life or because she cannot imagine what might become of such a person.

Moreover, in two ways the form of the novel suggests the impossibility of creating an identity outside of social relations. First, Morrison analogizes Shadrack's fear of death to the community's fear of Sula in order to examine the human need to name the things that defy categorization. Shadrack, the insane First World War veteran whose story opens the novel, exemplifies in the extreme this need to explain or find a place for the inexplicable. He has been driven mad by the grotesque way in which one of his comrades was killed. One minute they were marching routinely. The next minute shellfire exploded around them. The narrator tells us: "He turned his head a little to the right and saw the face of a soldier near him fly off. Before he could register shock, the rest of the soldier's head disappeared under the inverted soup bowl of his helmet. But stubbornly, taking no direction from the brain, the body of the headless soldier ran on, with energy and grace, ignoring altogether the drip and slide of brain tissue down its back" (p. 7). The sudden violence of this death has given Shadrack an unnatural fear of the unexpected; he is convinced, for example, that at any minute his hands will grow into monstrosities and that he will cease to exist. By creating National Suicide Day, he finds a way of controlling his fear: "If one day a year were devoted to [death], everybody could get it out of the way and the rest of the year would be safe and free" (p. 12).

The people of the Bottom in Medallion, Ohio (the black community in which Sula and Shadrack live), ridicule Shadrack's holiday, but their survival, like his, depends on finding ways to control their fears. Superstitious beliefs, which recur in the narrative and in their collective discourse, help them explain disturbing disruptions. When Hannah, Sula's mother, dies suddenly, Sula's grandmother, Eva, reflects that she would have been prepared for the tragedy if she had read properly the omens she had received. Likewise the denizens of the Bottom remark that they should have anticipated Sula's deleterious effect on their community because her unexpected return after a ten-year absence was accompanied by a plague of robins. Like Eva, the townspeople find a sign or a reason for their trouble after the fact. Their retrospective justifications are finally no different from Shadrack's.

Just as they must find a way to control the unexpected evils that beset them, so do they find a place for Sula. Since they do not understand her, they call her evil and hold her responsible for the injuries and deaths that befall their community.[7] As the narrator notes, the townspeople actually become more generous and better behaved when they shun Sula because they attach to her their own base impulses. For all her efforts to transcend the community, then, Sula remains an integral part of it.

In addition, Morrison undercuts Sula's sense of originality by characterizing her as only half a person. As several critics have argued, Sula and Nel complement each other psychologically; neither is fully herself after Sula's departure, and when she returns, her relationship with Nel's husband, Jude, further separates them.[8]

Sula and Nel are products of two different styles of upbringing. Their friendship grows out of their fascination with their dissimilarities. Sula's family is the source of her independence of mind and sexual nonchalance. Her mother is known for her sexual generosity and her grandmother for having sold her own leg under mysterious circumstances in order to provide for her children. Eva's home offers a figure for her family, replete with an ever-changing cast of boarders, gentleman callers, and foundlings: "Sula Peace lived in a house of many rooms that had been built over a period of five years to the specifications of its owner, who kept on adding things: more stairways—more rooms, doors and stoops. There were rooms that had three doors, others that opened out on the porch only and were inaccessible from any other part of the house; others that you could get to only by going through somebody's bedroom" (p. 26).

Nel, by contrast, is raised in a well-ordered but repressive household and is thus prepared to choose the life of limited options that she shares with Jude. Haunted by the image of her own mother, a prostitute, Nel's mother tries to launder the "funk" out of her daughter's life. During their childhood and adolescence, Nel provides Sula with restraints, and Sula offers Nel courage. More important, they offer each other a kind of security that neither finds in her own family. Together they begin to discover the meaning of death and sexuality. As the narrator states:

> Because each had discovered years before that they were neither white nor male, and that all freedom and triumph were forbidden to them, they had set about creating something else to be. Their meeting was fortunate, for it let them use each other to grow on. Daughters of distant mothers and incomprehensible fathers (Sula's because he was dead; Nel's because he wasn't), they found in each other's eyes the intimacy they were looking for.
>
> (pp. 44–45)

Their relationship is permanently destroyed when Sula sleeps with Jude, although Sula reflects that she never intended to cause Nel pain. Without Nel, "the closest thing to both an other and a self" (p. 103), Sula is cut off from the only relationship that gives her life meaning and so drifts toward her death. Nel too is rendered incomplete when her friendship with Sula dissolves. She may think that her inescapable grief is the result of having lost her husband, but as she realizes at the end of the novel, what she has missed for so many years was not Jude but Sula.

The descendant of a line of relatively autonomous women, Sula attempts to go them one better and create herself outside the collective assumptions about women's behavior. Morrison denies the feasibility of such a choice most obviously by killing her protagonist off. But the narrative structures she employs in *Sula* further undercut Sula's aspirations. By characterizing her as both a communal scapegoat and the second self of her more conventional best friend, Morrison denies Sula the originality she seeks.

৯৯

In *Sula* and *The Bluest Eye* Morrison uses flashbacks and interpolated stories in order to show how broadly shared values simultaneously contribute to and subvert the construction of identity. But, as I have suggested, both novels focus on the implications of a specified cultural and political condition. *The Bluest Eye* uses the technique to examine the consequences of measuring oneself by alien standards; *Sula* considers the ways in which society denies women the possibility of autonomy and independence. In contrast, *Song of Solomon* presents a character whose identity depends on his discovery of a narrative.

The narrative of *Song of Solomon*, like the narrative of *The Bluest Eye* and *Sula*, proceeds in a nonlinear fashion. Although we see Milkman, or Macon Dead III, the protagonist, moving from childhood to adulthood, his story is interrupted repeatedly by flashbacks from other characters' lives that suspend the narrative line. Indeed, most of the characters in the novel have a story to tell. Some narrate their tales spontaneously; some must be provoked into telling them. Some stories contradict, some complement each other. But virtually every important character tells a story from his or her past that both helps to explain present circumstances and impedes the forward progress of the central narrative.

Shortly before Milkman travels to the South to look for the gold his father believes Pilate stole from him when they were children, he remarks that he is beginning to "feel himself emerge, a clean-lined definite self."[9] He is certain that if he can find the gold, he will find himself, because then he will have a story to share with the other men in his community:

"He could tell this [the story of the gold]. The only other real confrontation he'd had was hitting his father, but that wasn't the kind of story that stirred the glitter up in the eyes of the old men at Tommy's" (p. 185). In fact, Milkman's achieving personal fulfillment—identity—is determined by his finding a story to tell. Like Bigger Thomas and the invisible man, he needs to understand and accept his past before he can know the meaning of his identity. Morrison suggests, however, that to tell the story of a single adventure, or even of his life, will not adequately define him. The communal sense of identity that informs the earlier novels obtains here as well. Milkman's search for self-fulfillment is complete only when he recognizes that identity is a collective rather than an individual construct, and so defines himself in relation to a broad sense of history and community. That is, until Milkman learns to tell his family's story—or, to be more exact, to sing his family's song—his search for himself remains incomplete.

The Dead family, the focus of *Song of Solomon,* is composed of two branches that might be distinguished by the ways in which they perceive time and personal relationships. The Macon Dead, Jr., branch, Milkman's immediate family, describes time in a linear way, indeed wants to repudiate the past, and objectifies personal relationships. His Aunt Pilate Dead's family, in contrast, describes time cyclically and cherishes relationships. Milkman's development might be described as a movement from a linear to a cyclical perspective on experience.[10] When he is able to appreciate the values he associates with his aunt, he achieves emotional fulfillment and understands the necessity of singing the family song.

The Macon Deads exemplify the patriarchal, nuclear family that has traditionally been a stable and critical feature of Western civilization. The misery of their daily lives demonstrates how few guarantees that domestic configuration actually carries. Macon, Jr., son of an American Adam who loved the soil and worked it brilliantly, inherited only some of his father's talent. Able to "work" only cash, he lacks the organic connection to the soil that the novel suggests saved Macon, Sr., from the obsessive, dehumanizing materialism that drives his son. Macon's primary goal is to amass a fortune and a business he can bequeath to his only son, Milkman, who is the most important person in his life. Macon believes him to be the vehicle through which his empire, his spirit, and thus his line will continue to live. He therefore essentially dismisses anyone who either obstructs or fails to contribute to his progress; his faith is in the acquisition of things, not in the development of human relations. As he tells Milkman in childhood: "Come to my office; work a couple of hours there and learn what's real. Let me tell you right now the one important thing you'll ever need to know: Own things. And let the things you own own other things. Then you'll own yourself and other people too" (p. 55).

Macon's proprietary impulse informs his treatment of other people. His eviction of Mrs. Bains reveals his insensitivity to his tenants; to him they are but so much property. This lack of sympathy extends beyond business to his relationships with his family. Macon brutalizes his wife, Ruth, both subtly and overtly, because he suspects her of incestuous relations with her father and son. Macon recalls that while his father-in-law, Dr. Foster, was alive, father and daughter were united in opposition against him. He objected when Dr. Foster served as his own daughter's obstetrician and was outraged years later when he entered the doctor's bedroom to discover this scene: "In the bed. That's where she was when I opened the door. Laying next to him. Naked as a yard dog, kissing him. Him dead and white and puffy and skinny, and she had his fingers in her mouth" (p. 73). Moreover, he intuits rightly that his son's nickname, "Milkman," may refer to the length of time he was breast-fed.

Macon treats his other relatives with scarcely more consideration than he shows Ruth. His egocentricity motivates his concern for Milkman, the only person in whom he seems to have any real interest. As Macon himself remarks, despite his concern for him, he can speak to his son only "if his words [hold] some command or criticism": " 'Hello Daddy.' 'Hello, son, tuck your shirt in.' 'I found a dead bird, Daddy.' 'Don't bring that mess in this house . . .' " (p. 29). Like everyone else in the family, Macon has no use for his daughters, Lena and Corinthians. The two are introduced in the novel as "half grown, scrambling about in the snow trying to catch the red velvet rose petals" (p. 5). This description confronts the reader with a paradox invoked repeatedly throughout the novel: the family always treats these two women as if they were still children.

By refusing to acknowledge his sister Pilate, Macon objectifies her as well. His resentment is based in part on his belief that she has stolen some gold that the two of them should have shared. More significantly, however, he eschews her company because he considers her deportment socially unacceptable. He fears that the white bankers will cease to trust him if they associate him with a bootlegging woman.

Weak and pathetic as she is, Ruth Dead finds subtle methods of objectifying her husband as well. She attracts her husband's attention in the only way available to her: she manipulates him until he feels that he has no choice but to beat or humiliate her. She remarks that Milkman too has never been "a person to her": "Because she had been so desperate to lie with her husband and have another baby by him, the son she bore was first off a wished-for bond between her and Macon, something to hold them together and reinstate their sex lives" (p. 130). Realizing that her husband will never again provide her with sexual affection, she obtains gratification from her son by breast-feeding him until he is old enough to talk, stand up, and wear knickers.

The singleness of purpose that afflicts Macon and the members of his family is at least partly responsible for their cruelty to each other. It causes them to construct strict divisions—such as those between self and other—in terms of which they view the world. Moreover, this rigidity of vision extends to their perception of time. Trapped in a specific moment, they deny the interrelatedness of past, present, and future. Ruth escapes her grim, empty marriage by living almost entirely in the past. For years she has slept on her father's grave to recapture "that cared-for feeling that [she] got from him" because "he cared whether and he cared how [she] lived, and there was, and is, no one else in the world who ever did" (p. 124).

Macon, by contrast, lives entirely for the future. Believing himself to be a type of the self-made man, he acknowledges past debts to no one. He measures himself and his worth in terms of what he possesses in the present and what it will bring him in the future. His rejection of Pilate typifies his alienation from his past. Despite his devotion to her as a child, Macon turns his back on her at precisely the point when money becomes more important to him than kinship.

Macon and Ruth Dead are among the least effective storytellers in the novel, perhaps because neither can move imaginatively from one moment in time to another. They are reluctant to tell their tales. Macon, for example, discusses his past only when provoked. Occupied with the business of getting and spending, he has neither an audience for nor an interest in his stories: "When he was first married he used to talk about Lincoln's Heaven to Ruth. Sitting on the porch swing in the dark, he would re-create the land that was to have been his. Or when he was just starting out in the business of buying houses, he would lounge around the barbershop and swap stories with the men there. But for years he hadn't had that kind of time, or interest" (pp. 51–52). He tells his son about his own boyhood and his parents only after Milkman has disobeyed him and visited Pilate. He explains his hatred of Ruth only after Milkman has hit him. And he articulates his anger at Pilate as a way of getting Milkman to steal her gold. Similarly, Ruth tells Milkman about her love for her father only after he discovers her in the cemetery. For both husband and wife the past is hidden.

Moreover, as their conflicting versions of Ruth's obsession with her father indicate, the stories they do tell tend ultimately to fragment rather than cement relationships. Macon says that he saw his nude wife in bed with her father's corpse, sucking his fingers. According to Ruth, however, she wore a slip, knelt beside her father's bed, and kissed his fingers because they were the only unbloated part of his body. The difference between the two versions is representative of the distance between Ruth and Macon. Reliving the past is yet another means they have of isolating themselves from each other.

Like her brother, Pilate Dead presides over a predominantly female household. And like him she is self-made. But while Macon is trapped by his love of property and his business relationships, Pilate is free of such restraints. The lore surrounding Pilate's birth suggests her independence and capacity for self-creation: as the family legend has it, she was born after her mother's death, without a navel.

Throughout her life her smooth stomach isolates her from community, since those who know the legend shun her. Yet Pilate's situation is different from Sula's, for while Sula's independence seems purposeless, Pilate conscientiously chooses a set of values by which she lives. Her enforced isolation prompts her to "throw away every assumption she had learned and [begin] at zero" (p. 149). She discovers that for her it is not material possessions but her spirituality and magical abilities that constitute what is real. She decides for herself what is important and remakes herself accordingly.

While the Macon Deads' vision of the world is linear, rigid, and exclusionary, Pilate sees the world in a cyclical, expansive, non-Western manner. Because personal relationships are more important to her than material acquisitions, she supports others with her emotional generosity. The Macon Dead household may be barren and lifeless, but Pilate's home bursts with energy, sensuality, and affection. Pilate, her daughter, Reba, and her granddaughter, Hagar, are always engaged in some activity, often singing together spontaneously. On his way to his own emotionally empty house one evening, Macon, Jr., goes out of his way to peek through his sister's window in search of spiritual nourishment. He hears the three women singing a song, sees Pilate stirring the contents of a pot, Reba clipping her toenails, and Hagar braiding her hair. Macon is comforted both by the constant, soothing motion of each character in the vignette and by the harmony and tranquillity of their music.

Macon and Ruth understand neither each other nor their children. Their egocentricity prevents them from seeing beyond their own narrow, private perspective. Pilate, by contrast, transcends her individual identity and responds to other people's troubles as if they were her own. She suffers when she learns that Hagar may have known spiritual hunger, and threatens to kill a man who strikes Reba. Her compassion extends beyond her immediate family as well, for Pilate does not seem to distinguish between "inside" and "outside." She refuses, for example, to acknowledge the difference between a brother and a cousin, saying, "You treat them both the same" (p. 44).

Indeed, although she is estranged from Macon, she repeatedly comes to his family's aid. She uses her magical powers to rekindle temporarily his sexual passion, and to allow Ruth to protect Milkman, the child who results from that temporary union. She opens her home to her nephew and rescues him and his friend Guitar from jail even after they have tried to rob her. Her dying words testify to her boundless compassion: "I wish I'd a knowed more people. I would of loved 'em all. If I'd a knowed more, I would a loved more" (p. 340).

Another consequence of Pilate's expansive vision is her cyclical, mythic vision of time. She believes that one can never escape one's past, that it exists in dynamic relationship to the present. She therefore carries her history with her in the form of her songs, her rocks, her bag of bones, and her stories. To her mind, one's sense of identity is rooted in the capacity to look back to the past and synthesize it with the present; it is not enough to put the past behind and look forward. As she tells Macon: "You can't take a life and walk off with it. Life is life. Precious. And the dead you kill is yours. They stay with you anyway, in your mind. So it's a better thing, a more better thing to have the bones right there with you wherever you go. That way, it frees up your mind" (p. 210).

Inasmuch as Macon's and Ruth's rigidity makes them poor storytellers, Pilate's flexibility renders her a consummate narrator. She is always ready to tell a story because the past is always with her. During their first meeting, for example, Pilate tells Milkman three stories.[11] Moreover, unlike Macon's stories, which tend to fracture relationships, Pilate's tales bring them together. Milkman feels "completely happy" (p. 47) for the first time in his life when he listens to stories in her house. And the story she tells about the bones that hang in her house bring about Milkman's and Guitar's release from jail.

The most important story Pilate tells—the fragmented lyrics of the Song of Solomon—is, ironically, one she neither knows to be a story nor knows completely. When she sings her incomplete version of the Song of Solomon, Pilate seems uninterested in its narrative line. For her and her family its value is entirely curative, bringing them together in moments of pain, such as the time when Hagar confesses that she has been "hungry" (pp. 48–49). Its meaning is crucial to Milkman, however, for it provides him with a context within which his life assumes significance.

While he lives in Michigan, Milkman sees the world as a linear and rigid structure, as his father does. Generally egocentric and unsympathetic, Milkman helps other people only when his arrogance motivates him to do so. For example, he believes that he hit his father in order to protect Ruth. In fact, as Lena rightly tells him: "You think because you hit him once that we all believe you were protecting her. Taking her side. It's a lie. You were taking over, letting us know you had the right to tell her and all of us what to do" (p. 217). Similarly, lacking all awareness of Corinthians's loneliness, he disrupts her affair with the janitor Porter because he thinks his sister is too good for him. Lena again identifies the selfishness inherent in his intervention:

What do you know about somebody not being good enough for someone else? And since when did you care whether Corinthians stood up or fell down? You've been laughing at us all your life. Corinthians. Mama. Me. Using us, ordering us, and judging us: how we cook your food; how we keep your house. But now all of a sudden, you have Corinthians' welfare at heart and break her up

from a man you don't approve of. Who are you to approve
or disapprove anybody or anything?   (p. 216)

His letter to Hagar reveals his inability to move beyond the
limits of his ego to understand her feelings and psychology.
While they were lovers, he treated her carelessly; when he
decides to leave her, he fails to accept responsibility for ending their relationship. Instead he writes her little more than a
business letter, in which he suggests that he has left her for
her own good:

> I'll remind her that we are cousins, he thought . . . That he
> was not what she needed. She needed a steady man who
> could marry her. He was standing in her way. And since
> they were related and all, she should start looking for
> someone else. It hurt him, he would say, deeply hurt him,
> after all these years, but if you loved somebody as he did
> her, you had to think of them first . . . [Milkman] wrote
> Hagar a nice letter which ended: "Also, I want to thank
> you. Thank you for all you have meant to me. For mak-
> ing me happy all these years. I am signing this letter with
> love, of course, but more than that, with gratitude."
> (pp. 98–99)

At this stage in his life Milkman, like his father, values
material possessions above relationships. He goes to the
South in search of gold because he believes that wealth will
enable him to escape his family and his past and thereby
assure him of emotional fulfillment: "Command. That was
what he wanted in his life . . . He just wanted to beat a path
away from his parents' past . . . which was threatening to
become his present" (pp. 180–181).

This desire to run from the past makes Milkman a poor
storyteller. Indeed, until he travels south he has no story at

all. He cannot, for example, tell Guitar clearly and lucidly what transpired between him and his father. He needs his friend to straighten out the sequence of events and fill in the gaps in his story:

"What'd she do Milk?"
"Nothin. Smiled. He didn't like her smile."
"You're not making sense. Talk sense. And slow
down. You know you can't hold liquor."
"What you mean, I can't hold liquor?"
" 'Scuse me. Help yourself."
"I'm trying to have a serious conversation and you
talking shit, Guitar."
"I'm listening."
"And I'm talking."
"Yes, you talking, but what are you saying?"

(pp. 86–87)

His fear of the past also makes him a bad listener. Perhaps because he cannot escape her magic, Milkman enjoys Pilate's stories. But he prefers not to listen to other people's tales. He doesn't want to hear Guitar's story of how he came to value human and animal life ("Oh, shit, do we have to hear about Alabama again?" (p. 85) and therefore does not understand its applicability to his own life: "Milkman nodded his head [after the story had ended], but it was clear to Guitar that nothing he had said had made any difference. Chances were Milkman didn't even know what a doe was, and whatever it was, it wasn't his mother" (p. 86). Similarly, he is profoundly disturbed by his father's story of his marriage. He does not want to know about his mother's relationship to her father. And he most definitely does not want to remember that he was breast-fed until he was old enough to wear knickers:

"Goddam," Milkman said aloud. "What the fuck did he tell me all that shit for?" He didn't want to know any of it. There was nothing he could do about it. The doctor was dead. You can't do the past over.

Milkman's confusion was rapidly turning to anger. "Strange motherfuckers," he whispered. "Strange." If he wanted me to lay off, he thought, why didn't he just say that? Just come to me like a man and say, Cool it. You cool it and I'll cool it. We'll both cool it. And I'd say, Okay, you got it. But no. He comes to me with some way-out tale about how come and why.   (p. 76)

Although Milkman seems determined to reject the past, part of him remains fascinated by it. Even as a child he cannot escape his history altogether: "It was becoming a habit—this concentration on things behind him" (p. 35). This subliminal fascination with the past enables him to respond to and ultimately adopt the values upheld by "his people" in the South. Milkman's assumption that the key to his liberation may be found there is correct, although it is not gold that will free him. In Danville and Shalimar, the part of the South from which his family comes, communal, mythical values prevail over individualistic, materialistic ones; by learning to see life according to this new (to him) set of assumptions, he arrives at an understanding of what his experience means.

Milkman travels south wearing a "beige three-piece suit, button down light-blue shirt and black string tie, beautiful Florsheim shoes," and a gold Longines watch (pp. 228–229). He ruins and loses various articles of clothing and jewelry as he searches first for the gold and then for the story of his people. Indeed, just before his epiphany during the bobcat hunt—the moment when he recognizes his connection to the lives of his friends and relatives—he changes out of his cosmopolitan attire into overalls and brogans. Similarly, the people he meets in Shalimar and Danville force him to throw off his pretenses before they offer him help and information. Only when he ceases to flaunt his wealth and refer casually to their women do they admit him into their community. Until he sheds the leaden trappings of materialism, Milkman, like the peacock he and Guitar encounter, is too weighted down by his vanity to fly.

The values Milkman adopts in the South are precisely those that Pilate represents. Indeed, as he develops a sense of himself, he becomes more his aunt's heir than his father's. In his youth Milkman believed that when he had finally achieved his freedom, he would no longer need to submit to the claims of others. In the woods, away from the destructive effects of civilization, however, he realizes that connectedness is an inescapable part of humanity:

> It sounded old. *Deserve.* Old and tired and beaten to death. Deserve. Now it seemed to him that he was always saying or thinking that he didn't deserve some bad luck, or some bad treatment from others. He'd told Guitar that he didn't "deserve" his family's dependence, hatred, or whatever. That he didn't even "deserve" to hear all the misery and mutual accusations his parents unloaded on him. Nor did he "deserve" Hagar's vengeance. But why shouldn't his parents tell him their personal problems? If not him, then who? . . .
>
> Apparently he thought he deserved only to be loved— from a distance, though—and given what he wanted. And in return he would be . . . what? Pleasant? Maybe all he was really saying was: I am not responsible for your pain; share your happiness with me but not your unhappiness.
>
> (pp. 279–280)

Formerly, he had tried to avoid responsibility for his actions as a way of distancing himself from his past. In Shalimar, however, he discovers a capacity for understanding his parents' feelings, and a sense of shame for having stolen from Pilate. This newly acquired compassion allows him to confront his past experiences with a degree of directness that was unavailable to him previously.

> The skim of shame that he had rinsed away in the bathwater after having stolen from Pilate returned. But now it was as thick and as tight as a caul. How could he have broken into that house—the only one he knew that achieved comfort without one article of comfort in it. No soft worn-down chair, not a cushion or a pillow. No light switch, no water running free and clear after a turn of a tap handle. No napkins, no tablecloth. No fluted plates or flowered cups, no circle of blue flame burning in a stove eye. But peace was there, energy, singing, and now his own remembrances.   (p. 304)

In keeping with this new awareness of other people and of his past, Milkman, insensitive to Hagar and unwilling to assume responsibility for her while she was alive, understands her now that she is dead, and he assumes the burden of her death. He acknowledges the inappropriateness of his letter to her and realizes that he has used her. Moreover, he knows even without being told that she is dead and he is to blame. As Pilate has carried with her the bones of the man she believes she has murdered, so too does Milkman resolve to carry with him the box containing Hagar's hair as a symbol of the past he no longer needs to escape.

Milkman's transformation is a direct result of the stories he hears in the South. At first he solicits the tales simply because he hopes to learn where Pilate's gold is hidden. He soon discovers, however, that the stories provide him with a more substantial sense of history and reality than he has ever known. By anchoring him solidly in place and in time, they enable him to feel a coherent, genuine sense of self as well as a profound commitment to others. He recognizes that hearing Reverend Cooper talk about his family, for example, provides him with a new security: "Milkman felt a glow listening to a story come from this man he'd heard many times before but only half listened to. Or maybe it was being there in the place where it happened that made it seem so real . . . Here in the parsonage, sitting in a cane-bottom chair near an upright piano and drinking homemade whiskey poured from a mayonnaise jar, it was real" (p. 233).

The information about his ancestors brings his own life into focus. Learning about his grandfather's character helps him understand what his father meant when he said that he worked beside him. But even more significant, listening to the stories binds him into a relationship with the community of tellers. He feels at one even with eccentrics such as Grace Long and Susan Byrd:

> He was curious about these people. He didn't feel close to them, but he did feel connected, as though there was some cord or pulse or information they shared. Back home he had never felt that way, as though he belonged to any-place or anybody. He'd always considered himself the out-sider in his family, only vaguely involved with his friends, and except for Guitar, there was no one whose opinion of himself he cared about . . . But there was something he felt now—here in Shalimar, and earlier in Danville—that re-minded him of how he used to feel in Pilate's house. Sit-ting in Susan Byrd's living room, lying with Sweet, eating with those men at Vernell's table, he didn't have to get over, to turn on, or up, or even out. (p. 296)

For Milkman's people, then, story telling does more than bring one's individual past into relation with the present. It is also, perhaps more important, a community-building ritual. The stories Reverend Cooper, Circe, and Susan Byrd tell Milkman are only ostensibly their own; taken together they tell Milkman the collective story of his ancestors. Story telling is therefore shown to bind tellers and listeners and individual stories into a collective unit.

It is particularly appropriate that in this rural enclave the stories are communal, since they arise out of a sense of group identity. The capacity for gestures of generosity and connection is more highly valued than self-protective, proprietary impulses. That the stories bind people to one another, and that Milkman understands himself in relation to others after hearing them, further indicates that the individual life in Shalimar and Danville acquires its meaning in relationship to other lives.

Milkman has no story, and therefore no identity in Michigan. In the South, however, he acquires a tale—the story of his ancestors—that even Pilate has only partially known. Milkman delights in singing the family song. Moreover, he anticipates sharing it with "his people" at home in Michigan, because the song contains his history and therefore the meaning of his life. That Milkman can accept the family story as his own, becoming most himself after comprehending it, further symbolizes his development beyond the constraints of his earlier egocentricity. The most powerful evidence of Milkman's effectiveness as a storyteller, however, is his ability to use the song curatively. Throughout the novel the best narrators—Pilate and the southerners—use their songs and stories to reach out to others. When Milkman eases Pilate's dying by singing his song to her, he shows that he can put his story to use for others as well as for himself.

The act of flight has always been a subliminal part of Milkman's life. His birth was precipitated by the abortive attempt at flight of one Robert Smith. As a child he disliked riding backward because it reminded him of "flying blind, and not knowing where he [was] going" (p. 31). And later, as he approaches Circe's house, he recalls his childhood fantasy of being able to fly. After Milkman understands the song, however, it becomes clear (certainly to the reader if not explicitly to Milkman himself) that his fascination with flight is an inherited affinity. His final leap into the air recalls his great-grandfather's flight and proves that he understands his history and has made it his own.[12]

❧

In an interview conducted while she was writing *Song of Solomon,* Morrison suggested that she intended Guitar Bains to provide a contrast to Milkman. One character, she said, presumably referring to Guitar, is "truly masculine in the sense of going out too far where you're not supposed to go and running where you're not supposed to go and running toward confrontations rather than away from them . . . The other," presumably Milkman, "will learn to be a complete person."[13]

Guitar's development seems unrelated to his own story-telling ability, but it provides nonetheless a noteworthy counterpoint to Milkman's. Guitar's childhood and youth differ radically from his friend's. Orphaned and abandoned at an early age, raised by his poor but strong-willed grandmother, he was unaccustomed to the luxury that cushioned Milkman's youth. When his father was mangled to death in a sawmill, his employer offered the children a sack of candy—divinity. This woefully inappropriate response awakened

Guitar's social conscience by causing him to recognize that easy solutions can never heal suffering.

Guitar's poverty and rootlessness enable him to become part of the community. He is at home at Feather's Pool Hall and Tommy's Barber Shop, while Milkman remains an outsider. Given the differences between their backgrounds and behavior, one would expect that of the two men, Guitar would be the one to adopt antimaterialistic, communal values. But because of his involvement in the Seven Days, a vigilante organization that seeks to redress acts of racial persecution, Guitar becomes increasingly rigid and brutal while Milkman develops flexibility and compassion.

Milkman can be said to move into mythical time and out of historical time as his sense of himself grows. Indeed, he finds himself at home in an ostensibly timeless world in which people (Circe, for example) seem to live forever, and where fixed distinctions between past and present break down. In contrast, Guitar's hold on historical time tightens as his commitment to the Days increases. They have vowed to avenge in kind and at random all racially motivated crimes against black people. This kind of rigidity—specifically this willingness to appropriate the oppressor's rules—imprisons Guitar and the other Days within the very system they attempt to subvert. Unlike Milkman, they will never transcend the limitations of linear, exclusionary vision because they have never learned to perceive the world in terms other than those that enslave them.

The presence of Guitar and the Days in *Song of Solomon* historicizes a novel that would otherwise seem profoundly ahistorical, marked as it is by the presence of compelling mythic, supernatural elements. While the chronology of the novel ranges loosely from the antebellum period through the 1960s, the specific details of the Days' vigilante justice locates the final third of the text in a particular historical moment.

The interplay between narrative modes in this novel recalls the hybrid quality of each novel considered in this study. *The Autobiography of an Ex-Colored Man* invokes the conventions of autobiography; *Native Son,* a neonaturalist work, contains more than its share of political theory and sociological analysis. *Invisible Man* not only simulates autobiography but also contains elements of the impressionist and surrealist literary traditions.

The modern and contemporary black writers examined here, like the slave narrators, seem to be drawn to the strategies of nonfiction, what Barbara Foley calls the "documentary mode in black literature."[14] My selection of texts has focused in particular on the significance of autobiography in recent black fiction. To demonstrate the pervasive influence of the one genre on the other, I have examined novels that imitate the structure of autobiography as well as those that revolve around characters who develop the capacity to tell their own stories.

The writers' general affinity for hybrid forms may well derive from their alienation from the ideological content of received literary conventions. Or it may reflect their sense of the cultural work that their fictional productions are required to perform. In either case, the significance of autobiography as form and as process in these works underscores the importance of naming oneself and shaping one's own story, whether orally or in writing, in a culture where the discourse and ideology are controlled by "the Other." The persistence within black literature of autobiography as a set of strategies returns us always to the antebellum narratives as a source of black prose; the texts remind us of the subversive potential of even the more formulaic liminal genres.

Notes

Introduction

1. David Walker, *Appeal in Four Articles* (Boston, 1830; rpt. New York: Arno Press, 1969), p. 37.

2. Frederick Douglass, *The Narrative of the Life of Frederick Douglass, An American Slave, Written by Himself,* ed. Benjamin Quarles (Cambridge, Mass.: Harvard University Press, 1973), p. 59. Subsequent references are to this edition and will be given in the text.

3. Robert Pattison, *On Literacy: The Politics of the Word from Homer to the Age of Rock* (New York: Oxford University Press, 1982), p. 136.

4. Ibid., p. vi.

5. See John Blassingame, *The Slave Community: Plantation Life in the Antebellum South* (New York: Oxford University Press, 1972), and Vincent Harding, *There Is a River: The Black Struggle for Freedom in America* (New York: Vintage Books, 1981).

6. Terry Eagleton, *Literary Theory: An Introduction* (Minneapolis: University of Minnesota Press, 1983), pp. 1–53, 194–217; see also Eagleton, *The Function of Criticism: From "The Spectator" to Post-Structuralism* (London: Verso/NLB, 1984), pp. 69–124; Frank Lentricchia, *Criticism and Social Change* (Chicago: University of Chicago Press, 1983), pp. 1–52, 113–163; and Edward W. Said, "Opponents, Audiences, Constituencies, and Community," Hayden White, "The Politics of Historical Interpretation: Discipline and De-Sublimation," and Stanley Cavell, "Politics as Opposed to What?" all in *The Politics of Interpretation,* ed. W. J. T. Mitchell (Chicago: University of Chicago Press, 1983), pp. 7–32, 119–143, and 181–202, respectively.

7. Henry Louis Gates, Jr., "Criticism in the Jungle," in *Black Literature and Literary Theory* (New York: Methuen, 1984), p. 6.

1. Form and Ideology in Three Slave Narratives

1. William L. Andrews, "The First Fifty Years of the Slave Narrative, 1760–1810," in *The Art of Slave Narrative: Original Essays in Criticism and Theory*, ed. John Sekora and Darwin T. Turner (Macomb, Ill.: Western Illinois University Press, 1982), p. 7.

2. Marion Wilson Starling, *The Slave Narrative: Its Place in American History* (Boston: G. K. Hall, 1981), pp. xvii–xviii; Dorothy Sterling, ed., *We Are Your Sisters: Black Women in the Nineteenth Century* (New York: W. W. Norton, 1984), pp. 3–4.

3. Sterling, *We Are Your Sisters*, p. 4. For a compelling discussion of ways in which the WPA narratives might be used, see Paul D. Escott, "The Art and Science of Reading WPA Slave Narratives," in *The Slave's Narrative*, ed. Charles T. Davis and Henry Louis Gates, Jr. (New York: Oxford University Press, 1985), pp. 40–48.

4. Starling, *The Slave Narrative*, pp. 226–232.

5. See James Olney's provocative discussion of this tension in " 'I Was Born': The Slave Narratives, Their Status as Autobiography and as Literature," *Callaloo*, 20 (Winter 1984), 46–73.

6. Henry Louis Gates, Jr., "Criticism in the Jungle," in *Black Literature and Literary Theory* (New York: Methuen, 1984), p. 5.

7. The narratives first emerge as a subject in critical literature in the 1970s. The nature of the commentary bespeaks their troublesomeness as a literary category more precisely than does their omission from earlier studies. Two seminal books, Stephen Butterfield's *Black Autobiography in America* (Amherst: University of Massachusetts Press, 1974) and Sidonie Ann Smith's *Where I'm Bound: Patterns of Slavery and Freedom in Black American Autobiography* (Westport, Conn.: Greenwood Press, 1974) explore the connections between the narratives and modern black autobiography. Neither acknowledges the characteristics of the narratives that distinguish them from either history or autobiography; both present an image of the narratives as a monolithic body of work.

More recent studies seek to establish the relationship of the accounts to the conditions out of which they arose. Frances Smith Foster's *Witnessing Slavery* (Westport, Conn.: Greenwood Press, 1979) and Starling's *Slave Narrative: Its Place in American History* contribute immeasurably to our understanding of the narratives in their political, cultural, and literary contest. Both provide detailed summaries of the themes and plots of the narratives, but neither discusses the common rhetorical structures that bind the texts as a genre.

H. Bruce Franklin in *The Victim as Criminal and Artist: Literature from the American Prison* (New York: Oxford University Press, 1978) and Houston A. Baker, Jr., in *The Journey Back: Issues in Black Literature and Criticism* (Chicago: University of Chicago Press, 1980), in contrast, demonstrate ways in which the texts respond to the ideological context in which they were produced. By analyzing the resonance and textual strategies of the Douglass and Jacobs narratives in the one case and of the Equiano and Douglass narratives in the other, they offer the most persuasive evidence of their literariness. To borrow Franklin's formulation (p. 7), by using methods that ordinarily illuminate our readings of classic texts, they make a strong argument for the narratives' subtlety and complexity.

8. See Starling, *The Slave Narrative*, p. 50; Andrews, "The First Fifty Years," pp. 9–10; and Foster, *Witnessing Slavery*, pp. 44–52. Paul Edwards locates Equiano's account in the context of contemporaneous works by Ignatius Sancho and Ottobah Cugoano. See his "Three West African Writers of the 1780s," in Davis and Gates, *The Slave's Narrative*, pp. 175–198.

9. Andrews, "The First Fifty Years," p. 8.

10. Ibid., p. 10.

11. Olaudah Equiano [Gustavus Vassa], *The Interesting Narrative of the Life of Olaudah Equiano, or Gustavus Vassa, the African, Written by Himself* (Leeds: James Nichols, 1814), p. iii. Subsequent references are to this edition and will be given in the text.

12. Daniel B. Shea, Jr., *Spiritual Autobiography in America* (Princeton: Princeton University Press, 1968), p. 87.

13. For a general discussion of patterns in spiritual autobiography, see ibid., pp. 87–110; and G. A. Starr, *Defoe and Spiritual Autobiography* (Princeton: Princeton University Press, 1965), pp. 3–50.

14. See Chinosole, " 'Tryin' To Get Over': Narrative Posture in Equiano's Autobiography," in Sekora and Turner, *The Art of Slave Narrative*, pp. 45–54; Andrews, "The First Fifty Years," pp. 19–22; and Baker, *The Journey Back*, pp. 15–22.

15. Susan Willis argues that slave narratives generally feature narrators who only partly comprehend their situation. See her essay "Crushed Geraniums: Juan Francisco Manzano and the Language of Slavery," in Davis and Gates, *The Slave's Narrative*, pp. 199–224.

16. Dickson J. Preston's recent biography contains information that suggests that Douglass concealed certain details about his lineage and childhood to render his condition more bleak, his achievements more remarkable. See his *Young Frederick Douglass: The Maryland Years* (Baltimore: Johns Hopkins University Press, 1980).

17. For a full discussion of this development see George M. Frederickson, *The Black Image in the White Mind: The Debate on Afro-American Character and Destiny, 1817–1914* (New York: Harper and Row, 1971).

18. George Gusdorf, "Conditions and Limits of Autobiography," in *Autobiography: Essays Theoretical and Critical*, ed. James Olney (Princeton: Princeton University Press, 1979), p. 29.

19. Franklin, *The Victim as Criminal and Artist*, pp. 8–24; Houston A. Baker, Jr., *Long Black Song: Essays in Black American Literature and Culture* (Charlottesville: University Press of Virginia, 1972), pp. 74–79; and Albert E. Stone, "Identity and Art in Frederick Douglass's *Narrative*," *College Language Association Journal*, 17 (December 1973), 202–210.

20. Nancy T. Clasby, "Frederick Douglass's *Narrative*: A Content Analysis," *College Language Association Journal*, 14 (March 1971), 243.

21. Stone, "Identity and Art," pp. 203–204.

22. Ibid., p. 210; Butterfield, *Black Autobiography in America*, pp. 66–67.

23. Baker, *The Journey Back*, pp. 36–46.

24. Annette Niemtzow, "The Problematic of Self in Autobiography: The Example of the Slave Narrative," in Sekora and Turner, *The Art of Slave Narrative*, pp. 98–104.

25. Robert B. Stepto, *From Behind the Veil: A Study of Afro-American Narrative* (Urbana, Ill.: University of Illinois Press, 1979), pp. 16–26.

26. Niemtzow, "The Problematic of Self," pp. 105–108.

27. Ibid.

28. Linda Brent [Harriet Jacobs], *Incidents in the Life of a Slave Girl* (New York: Harcourt Brace Jovanovich, 1973), p. 117. Subsequent references will be given in the text.

29. As I completed revisions of this discussion, I read Houston A. Baker, Jr.'s, *Blues, Ideology, and Afro-American Literature: A Vernacular Theory* (Chicago: University of Chicago Press, 1984). He too considers the significance of this image to Jacobs's account, but he focuses on Jacobs's ability to transform the economics of her oppression, whereas I concentrate on her use of received literary conventions.

30. Elaine Showalter, "Review Essay," *Signs*, 1 (1975), 435.

31. Only recently have scholars accepted the authenticity of Jacobs's account, thanks largely to Jean Fagan Yellin's meticulous and illuminating documentation of Jacobs's life and writing. See her essay "Texts and Contexts of Harriet Jacobs's *Incidents in the Life of a Slave Girl: Written by Herself*," in Davis and Gates, *The Slave's Narrative*, pp. 262–282. See also Yellin's edition of this text (Cambridge, Mass.: Harvard University Press, 1987).

32. Sandra M. Gilbert and Susan Gubar, *The Madwoman in the Attic* (New Haven: Yale University Press, 1979), pp. 3–104 passim.

33. Ibid., p. 23.

34. Ann Douglas, *The Feminization of American Culture* (New York: Avon Books, 1977), pp. 240–273 passim.

35. Susan Gubar, " 'The Blank Page' and the Issues of Female Creativity," in *Writing and Sexual Difference*, ed. Elizabeth Abel (Chicago: University of Chicago Press, 1982), p. 74.

36. See Showalter, "Review Essay," and Gilbert and Gubar, *The Madwoman in the Attic*. See also Patricia Meyer Spacks, *The Female Imagination* (New York: Knopf, 1975), p. 317, and Carolyn Heilbrun and Catharine Stimpson, "Theories of Feminist Criticism: A Dialogue," in *Feminist Literary Criticism*, ed. Josephine Donovan (Lexington, Ky.: University Press of Kentucky, 1975), p. 62.

37. See Elizabeth Abel, Marianne Hirsch, and Elizabeth Langland, eds., *The Voyage In: Fictions of Female Development* (Hanover, N.H.: University Press of New England, 1983), pp. 3–19.

38. I draw here on the vocabulary of recent feminist psychoanalytic theory, which revises traditional accounts of female psychosexual development. See Jean Baker Miller, *Toward a New Psychology of Women* (Boston: Beacon Press, 1976); Nancy Chodorow, *The Reproduction of Mothering: Psychoanalysis and the Sociology of Gender* (Berkeley: University of California Press, 1978); and Carol Gilligan, *In a Different Voice* (Cambridge, Mass.: Harvard University Press, 1982).

39. I acknowledge here my gratitude to Mary Helen Washington for pointing out to me this characteristic of the narratives.

40. William Wells Brown, *Narrative of William W. Brown* (Boston: The Anti-Slavery Office, 1847; rpt. New York: Arno Press, 1968), p. 105.

41. Niemtzow, "The Problematic of Self," pp. 105–106.

42. See Douglas, *The Feminization of American Culture*, p. 72.

43. See Tania Modleski, *Loving with a Vengeance: Mass-Produced Fantasies for Women* (New York: Archon Books, 1982), p. 17, and Janice Radway, *Reading the Romance: Women, Patriarchy, and Popular Literature* (Chapel Hill: University of North Carolina Press, 1984), p. 75.

44. See Douglas, *The Feminization of American Culture*, p. 12.

45. See Barbara Smith, "Notes for Yet Another Paper on Black Feminism, or Will the Real Enemy Please Stand Up," *Conditions: Five*, 3 (October 1978), 123–132. For further discussion of this issue see Paula Giddings, *When and Where I Enter: The Impact of Black Women on Race and Sex in America* (New York: William Morrow, 1984); Angela Davis, *Women, Race, and Class* (New York: Vintage Books, 1983); and Elizabeth V. Spelman, "Theories of Race and Gender: The Erasure of Black Women," *Quest*, 5 (1979), 36–62.

2. *Privilege and Evasion in* The Autobiography of an Ex-Colored Man

1. Richard Bjornson's term. See his essay "The Picaresque Identity Crisis," in *The Novel and Its Changing Form,* ed. R. G. Collins (Winnipeg: University of Manitoba Press, 1972), p. 16.

2. My analysis explores Johnson's literary debt to the structures of the slave narratives. See Robert B. Stepto's discussion of his revision of tropes borrowed from Booker T. Washington's *Up From Slavery* and W. E. B. Du Bois's *Souls of Black Folk,* in *From Behind the Veil: A Study of Afro-American Narrative* (Urbana, Ill.: University of Illinois Press, 1979), pp. 95–127.

3. See, for example, Steven Bronz, *Roots of Negro Social Consciousness: The 1920s: Three Harlem Renaissance Writers* (New York: Libra Books, 1964); Sterling Brown, *The Negro in American Fiction* (Washington, D.C.: Associates in Negro Folk Education, 1937); Hugh Gloster, *Negro Voices in American Fiction* (Chapel Hill: University of North Carolina Press, 1948); Nathan Huggins, *Harlem Renaissance* (New York: Oxford University Press, 1971); and David Littlejohn, *Black on White: A Critical Survey of Writing by American Negroes* (New York: Viking, 1969).

4. See Werner Sollors's discussion of the complementary representations of the ex-colored man and Johnson's autobiographical persona in *Beyond Ethnicity: Consent and Descent in American Culture* (New York: Oxford University Press, 1986), p. 171.

5. Joseph T. Skerrett, Jr., "Irony and Symbolic Action in James Weldon Johnson's *The Autobiography of an Ex-Colored Man,*" *American Quarterly,* 32 (Winter 1980), 540–558.

6. James Weldon Johnson, *Along This Way: The Autobiography of James Weldon Johnson* (New York: Viking Press, 1961), p. 138. Subsequent references will be given in the text.

7. James Weldon Johnson, *The Autobiography of an Ex-Colored Man* (New York: Hill and Wang, 1960), p. 6. Subsequent references are to this edition and will be given in the text.

8. W. E. B. Du Bois, *The Souls of Black Folk,* in *Three Negro Classics,* ed. John Hope Franklin (New York: Avon Books, 1965), p. 215.

9. Stepto, *From Behind the Veil,* pp. 113–114.

10. Du Bois, *The Souls of Black Folk,* p. 221.

11. Skerrett and Marvin P. Garrett also comment on the counterpoint between creativity and capitalism in the novel. See Skerrett, "Irony and Symbolic Action," p. 556, and Garrett, "Early Recollections and Structural Irony in *The Autobiography of an Ex-Colored Man,*" *Critique,* 13 (Summer 1971), 5–14.

3. Alienation and Creativity in the Fiction of Richard Wright

1. Wright details his disaffection with the party in the second volume of his autobiography, *American Hunger,* written at the same time as *Black Boy* but not published until 1977.

2. See Katherine Fishburn, *Richard Wright's Hero: The Faces of a Rebel–Victim* (Metuchen, N.J.: Scarecrow Press, 1977).

3. Jackson is one of Wright's few middle-class protagonists. He is also the least imaginative, and may well be the least isolated. He seems to enjoy the company of his three friends and co-workers, Bob, Al, and Slim, but the physical condition of each of these men (one is consumptive, one obese, one syphilitic) suggests that these associations may be problematic.

4. Richard Wright, *The Outsider* (New York: Harper and Row, 1965), pp. 4 and 8, respectively.

5. Ibid., p. 439.

6. Donald B. Gibson makes a similar point. See *The Politics of Literary Expression: A Study of Major Black Writers* (Westport, Conn.: Greenwood Press, 1981), p. 50.

7. See, for example, Ralph Ellison, "Richard Wright's Blues," in *Shadow and Act* (New York: Random House, 1972), pp. 83–94; Gibson, "Richard Wright," pp. 41–42; George Kent, "Richard Wright: Blackness and the Adventure of Western Culture," in *Blackness and the Adventure of Western Culture* (Chicago: Third World Press, 1972), pp. 80–88; and Claudia C. Tate, *"Black Boy:* Richard Wright's 'Tragic Sense of Life,' " *Black American Literature Forum,* 10 (Winter 1976), 117–119.

8. Throughout his biography of Wright, Michel Fabre suggests that his troubled relation to his mother informed his attachments to other women and, by extension, the male-female relationships represented in his fiction. See *The Unfinished Quest of Richard Wright* (New York: William Morrow, 1973). See also Diane Long Hoeveler, "Oedipus Agonistes: Mothers and Sons in Richard Wright's Fiction," *Black American Literature Forum,* 12 (Summer 1978), 65–68.

9. In his discussion of the limits of protest fiction Ellison has written, "Wright could imagine Bigger, but Bigger could not possibly imagine Richard Wright." See "The World and the Jug," in *Shadow and Act,* p. 114. Robert B. Stepto makes a similar observation in *From Behind the Veil: A Study of Afro-American Narrative* (Urbana, Ill.: University of Illinois Press, 1979), pp. 148–149.

10. Richard Wright, *Black Boy: A Record of Childhood and Youth* (New York: Harper and Row, 1945), p. 10. Subsequent references are to this edition and will be cited in the text.

11. Richard Wright, *American Hunger* (New York: Harper and Row, 1977), p. 22.

12. Richard Wright, *Native Son* (New York: Harper and Row, 1966), p. 13. Subsequent references are to this edition and will be cited in the text.

13. Robert Bone argues as well that Bigger's kidnap note demonstrates his creative capacity. See his pamphlet *Richard Wright* (Minneapolis: University of Minnesota Press, 1969), p. 21.

14. Fishburn, *Richard Wright's Hero*, p. 7.

15. John M. Reilly, "Self-Portraits by Richard Wright," *The Colorado Quarterly*, 20 (1971), 45.

4. Ellison's Invisible Autobiographer

1. Ralph Ellison, "Brave New Words for a Startling Occasion," in *Shadow and Act* (New York: Random House, 1972), p. 103.

2. Ibid., p. 106.

3. Ralph Ellison, "The World and the Jug," in *Shadow and Act*, p. 114.

4. See Addison Gayle, Jr., *The Way of the New World: The Black Novel in America* (Garden City, N.Y.: Doubleday, 1976), pp. 246–258.

5. See Donald B. Gibson, *The Politics of Literary Expression: A Study of Major Black Writers* (Westport, Conn.: Greenwood Press, 1981), p. 93.

6. Houston A. Baker, Jr., "To Move without Moving: Creativity and Commerce in Ralph Ellison's Trueblood Episode," in *Black Literature and Literary Theory*, ed. Henry Louis Gates, Jr. (New York: Methuen, 1984), pp. 221–248.

7. See, for instance, Ralph Ellison, "The Art of Fiction: An Interview," in *Shadow and Act*, p. 167.

8. Ralph Ellison, *Invisible Man* (New York: Vintage, 1982), p. 16. Subsequent references are to this edition and will be cited in the text.

9. This incident in Bledsoe's past may well be a parody of Booker T. Washington's "entrance examination" for Hampton Institute, when he swept out a recitation room. See *Up from Slavery*, in *Three Negro Classics*, ed. John Hope Franklin (New York: Avon Books, 1965), pp. 56–57.

10. The phrase comes, of course, from W. E. B. Du Bois's landmark work, *The Souls of Black Folk*, in Franklin, *Three Negro Classics*, p. 215.

11. In Robert O'Meally's words, the invisible man learns that "history moves . . . like a boomerang: swiftly, cyclically, and dangerously . . . When he is not conscious of the past, he is liable to be slammed in the head with it when it circles back." See his book *The Craft of Ralph Ellison* (Cambridge, Mass.: Harvard University Press, 1980), p. 103.

12. O'Meally also sees this scene as a turning point in the invisible man's development. See ibid., p. 97.

13. Robert Stepto groups these mentors rather differently. See Robert B. Stepto, *From Behind the Veil: A Study of Afro-American Narrative* (Urbana, Ill.: University of Illinois Press, 1979), p. 177.

14. Trueblood's function in the novel has been the subject of critical debate. E. M. Kist argues that he is an opportunist, "a comic bumbler who cashes in on his pitiful situation by recounting it with broad irony and folk humor." See "A Langian Analysis of Blackness in Ralph Ellison's *Invisible Man*," *Studies in Black Literature*, 7 (1976), 23. For studies that evaluate Trueblood as a blues artist, see Raymond Olderman, "Ralph Ellison's Blues and *Invisible Man*," *Wisconsin Studies in Contemporary Literature*, 7 (1966), 146; George E. Kent, "Ralph Ellison and the Afro-American Folk and Cultural Tradition," in *Ralph Ellison: A Collection of Critical Essays*, ed. John Hersey (Englewood Cliffs, N.J.: Prentice-Hall, 1974), pp. 45–46; and Robert O'Meally, *The Craft of Ralph Ellison*, pp. 86–87.

15. Selma Fraiberg, "Two Modern Incest Heroes," *Partisan Review*, 5–6 (1961), 659.

16. O'Meally also notes that Trueblood's tale redeems his "absurd situation." See *The Craft of Ralph Ellison*, pp. 86–87.

17. Stepto also discusses Ellison's demystification of mentor figures in the novel. See *From Behind the Veil*, pp. 178–183.

18. Frank Kermode, *The Sense of an Ending: Studies in the Theory of Fiction* (New York: Oxford University Press, 1967), p. 17.

5. Toni Morrison's Narratives of Community

1. Much of the criticism of Toni Morrison's novels acknowledges this incompatibility between received assumptions and the texture and demands of life in Afro-American communities. See, for example, Joan Bischoff, "The Novels of Toni Morrison: Studies in Thwarted Sensitivity," *Studies in Black Literature*, 6 (1975), 21–23; Barbara Christian, *Black Women Novelists: The Development of a Tradition* (Westport, Conn.: Greenwood Press, 1980); Phyllis Klotman, "Dick-and-Jane and the Shirley Temple Sensibility in *The Bluest Eye*," *Black American Literature Forum*, 13 (1979), 123–125; and Susan Willis, "Eruptions of Funk: Historicizing Toni Morrison," in *Black Literature and Literary Theory*, ed. Henry Louis Gates, Jr. (New York: Methuen, 1984), pp. 263–285.

These essays are thematic in focus, concentrating on the political and psychological consequences of this type of cultural alienation. While I acknowledge the importance of these studies to our understanding of central issues in Morrison's writing, I am more interested in the ways in which her narrative forms enhance or subvert her thematic concerns.

2. Toni Morrison, *The Bluest Eye* (New York: Holt, Rinehart, and

Winston, 1970), p. 160. Subsequent references are to this edition and will be cited in the text.

3. What I describe here is a kind of narrative resonance that both confirms Pecola's story and calls attention to its representativeness. Barbara Christian has written about the resonant quality of Morrison's writing somewhat differently. She notes that Morrison expands the implications of Pecola's story by allowing her metaphors to reverberate. See Christian, *Black Women Novelists*, pp. 151–152.

4. Maureen's contempt for blackness is suggested by her summary of the plot of the movie *Imitation of Life*, which she says is about "this mulatto girl [who] hates her mother 'cause she is black and ugly but then cries at the funeral" (p. 57).

5. Toni Morrison, *Sula* (New York: Knopf, 1973), p. 105. Subsequent references are to this edition and will be cited in the text.

6. See Christian, *Black Women Novelists*, p. 171, and Faith Pullin, "Landscapes of Reality: The Fiction of Contemporary Afro-American Women," in *Black Fiction: New Studies in the Afro-American Novel since 1945*, ed. A. Robert Lee (New York: Harper and Row, 1980), pp. 195–196.

7. Both Barbara Christian and Philip M. Royster demonstrate that Sula functions as a communal scapegoat. See Christian, *Black Women Novelists*, pp. 164–165, and Royster, "A Priest and a Witch against The Spiders and The Snakes: Scapegoating in Toni Morrison's *Sula*," *Umoja*, n.s., 2 (Fall 1978), 149–168.

8. See, for example, Jane S. Bakerman, "Failures of Love and Female Initiation in the Novels of Toni Morrison," *American Literature*, 52 (January 1981), 549, and Christian, *Black Women Novelists*, pp. 161–162.

9. Toni Morrison, *Song of Solomon* (New York: New American Library, 1977), p. 184. Subsequent references are to this edition and will be cited in the text.

10. Bonnie Barthold describes the structure of the novel in similar terms. See her chapter on *Song of Solomon* in *Black Time* (New Haven: Yale University Press, 1981), pp. 174–184.

11. She tells him stories about his grandfather, about boiling an egg, and about a death resulting from an imagined fear.

12. Barthold notes that the act of flight also alludes to slave beliefs, "especially perhaps those of Ibo origin, that after death one's spirit would return to the home of the ancestors." See Barthold, *Black Time*, p. 176.

13. Robert Stepto, " 'Intimate Things in Place'—A Conversation with Toni Morrison," in *The Third Woman: Minority Women Writers of the United States*, ed. Dexter Fisher (Boston: Houghton Mifflin, 1980), p. 176.

14. Barbara Foley, "History, Fiction, and the Ground Between: The Uses of the Documentary Mode in Black Literature," *PMLA*, 95 (May 1980), 389–403.

Index

Andrews, William L., 9, 12–13
Angelou, Maya, 2

Baker, Houston A., Jr., 26–27, 89–90,
  157n7, 158n29
Barthold, Bonnie, 164nn10,12
Bildungsroman, 33
Bone, Robert, 162n13
Brown, William Wells, 34
Butterfield, Stephen, 24, 156n7

Child, L. Maria, 35, 37–40
Christian, Barbara, 164nn3,7
Craft, William and Ellen, 33
Cugoano, Ottobah, 157n8

Davis, Charles T., 156n3, 157nn8,15,
  158n31
Douglas, Ann, 30, 41
Douglass, Frederick, 3, 33, 36, 65,
  157nn7,16; *Narrative of the Life of
  Frederick Douglass*, 1–2, 3, 11–12, 20–
  28, 34–35; Captain Auld, 22, 23–24;
  Mrs. Auld, 23; Covey, 22, 25;
  Demby, 22; Grandmother, 22; Aunt
  Hester, 21, 23, 25; Plummer, 23;
  Master Thomas, 25
Du Bois, W. E. B., 1, 44, 56, 61, 66,
  160n2; *The Souls of Black Folk*, 44,
  57, 58, 66, 160n2

Edwards, Paul, 157n8
Ellison, Ralph, 7–8, 44, 69, 88–91,
  161n9, 163n17; "The Art of Fiction:
  An Interview," 162n7; "Brave
  Words for a Startling Occasion," 88,
  162n1; *Invisible Man*, 5, 44, 89–121,
  153, 162nn11,12; Homer A. Barbee,
  117, 118–120; Dr. Bledsoe, 91–92,
  94–97, 98–99, 116, 119, 162n9; The
  Brotherhood, 90, 101–109, 116; Tod
  Clifton, 104–106; Emerson, 98, 101;
  Grandfather, 91–92, 104, 107, 108,
  109; Jim Trueblood, 95–96, 109,
  110–115, 118, 163nn14,16; Ras the
  Exhorter, 107; Rinehart, 107–108;
  "The World and the Jug," 89,
  162n3
Equiano, Olaudah, 7, 26, 27, 33, 65,
  157nn7,8; *Narrative of the Life of
  Olaudah Equiano*, 12–20

Fabre, Michel, 161n8
Federal Writers' Project, 10
Fishburn, Katherine, 66, 86–87
Fisher, Dexter, 164n13
Foley, Barbara, 153
Foster, Frances Smith, 156n7
Fraiberg, Selma, 111
Franklin, H. Bruce, 157n7

Garrett, Marvin P., 160n11
Gates, Henry Louis, Jr., 6–7, 11,
  156n3, 157nn8,15, 158n31
Gayle, Addison, Jr., 89
Gibson, Donald B., 89, 161n6
Gilbert, Sandra, 30, 31
Gubar, Susan, 30, 31

Heilbrun, Carolyn, 31
Howe, Irving, 89

Imitation of Life (film), 164n4

Jacobs, Harriet, 7, 12, 65, 157n7,
  158nn29,31; *Incidents in the Life of a
  Slave Girl*, 12, 28–43, 158n31; Dr.
  Flint, 29, 32, 36–37, 41, 42; Grandmother, 32, 35, 43; Mr. Sands, 32–
  33, 41, 42
Johnson, James Weldon, 5, 7, 65–66,
  90, 160nn2,4; *Along This Way*, 45,
  47, 50; *Autobiography of an Ex-Colored
  Man*, 44–64, 91, 153, 160n11; *God's
  Trombones*, 48

Kermode, Frank, 120
Kist, E. M., 163n14

Malcolm X, 2
Modleski, Tania, 41
Morrison, Toni, 122–123, 135, 151,
  163n1, 164nn3,13; *The Bluest Eye*,
  123–130, 135; Pecola Breedlove,
  123–124, 125–126, 127–130, 164n3;
  Claudia MacTeer, 124, 125–127, 129;
  Frieda MacTeer, 127, 129; Geraldine,
  127–130; Junior, 127, 129; Maureen
  Peal, 127, 129–130, 164n4; Soaphead
  Church, 123–124; *Song of Solomon*, 5,
  8, 122–123, 135–151, 164n10; Guitar
  Bains, 142–143, 145, 147, 149, 151–
  152; Susan Byrd, 149, 150; Circe,
  150, 151, 152; Hagar, 141, 143, 144,
  147, 148; Macon Dead, Sr., 137, 149;
  Macon Dead, Jr., 135–140, 141, 142,
  143, 145–146; Milkman Dead, 5, 8,
  122, 135–152, 164n11; Pilate Dead,

136, 140–143, 145, 148, 150, 164n11;
  Ruth Dead, 137–140, 142, 145–146;
  Seven Days, 152; *Sula*, 123, 130–135,
  140, 164n7; Jude, 130, 133, 134; Nel,
  130, 133–134; Eva Peace, 132, 133;
  Hannah Peace, 132, 133; Shadrack,
  131–132; Sula Peace, 130–135, 140,
  164n7

Niemtzow, Annette, 26, 27, 28

Olderman, Raymond, 163n14
O'Meally, Robert, 162nn11,12

Pattison, Robert, 4
Preston, Dickson J., 157n16

Radway, Janice, 41
Reilly, John M., 87
Richardson, Samuel: *Pamela*, 36, 37, 41
Royster, Philip M., 164n7

Sancho, Ignatius, 157n8
Showalter, Elaine, 30, 31
Skerrett, Joseph T., Jr., 47, 160n11
Smith, Barbara, 43
Smith, Sidonie Ann, 156n7
Sollors, Werner, 160n4
Spacks, Patricia Meyer, 31
Starling, Marion Wilson, 10, 156n7
Stepto, Robert B., 58, 160n2, 161n9,
  163nn13,17, 164n13
Sterling, Dorothy, 10
Stimpson, Catharine, 31
Stone, Albert E., 23, 24

Vassa, Gustavus, *see* Equiano, Olaudah

Walker, David, 2
Washington, Booker T.: *Up from Slav-
  ery*, 160n2, 162n9
Washington, Mary Helen, 159n39
Wetmore, J. Douglass, 47, 50
Willis, Susan, 157n15
Works Progress Administration
  (WPA), 10, 156n3

Wright, Richard, 2, 66–70, 74–75, 86–
87, 89, 161nn8,9; *American Hunger,*
73–74, 87, 161n1; *Black Boy,* 66, 70–
72, 73, 87; *Eight Men,* 67, 87; *Lawd
Today,* 66, 67; *Long Dream, The,* 67,
68–69, 161n3; *Native Son,* 66, 68, 69,
75–87, 91, 153; Bessie, 75, 82, 83;
Buckley, 81–82, 84, 85–86; Mary

Dalton, 77–78, 80–81, 82, 85, 86;
Mr. and Mrs. Dalton, 76, 77, 80, 81;
Jan, 80–81, 82, 84–85; Max, 84, 86;
Bigger Thomas, 5, 8, 75–87, 91,
136, 162n13; *The Outsider,* 67–68, 69;
Uncle Tom's Children, 66, 67

Yellin, Jean Fagan, 158n31